Praise for The Law School Trip

MW00882026

"Laughter is what McClurg's ... ls
of undulating and ulul...
experience sparkle and ...
to make us laugh

— *The Law Teacher* (Fall 2001)

"[T]he quintessential book on the three years of torment and tribulation known as law school. ... [H]owlingly, gut-wrenchingly, turn purple and blow food out your nose funny! ... [S]hould be required reading for every law student and lawyer."

— *The Bimonthly Review of Law Books* (July-Aug 2001)

"[T]akes the sting right out of the high-handed pomposity, the double-talk, and officious seriousness of our legal training institutions ... [A] barrel of screwy fun ... [A] one of a kind piece of work that you don't have to be a lawyer or law student to love."

— *Text-Book.com*

"[D]ispense[s] buckets of advice without ever removing tongue from cheek. ... [A] 'loving parody' ... from the eyes of one who knows."

— *National Jurist, The Magazine for Law Students* (Jan. 2002)

"If your smart bone is connected to your funny bone, there's only one book for you: Andrew McClurg's *The Law School Trip*. It left me holding my sides while thinking: wait! I never *thought* about that before! This is *serious*! This book gave me more pure pleasure than anything I've read in months."

— Professor Marianne Wesson, bestselling author of *Render Up the Body* and *A Suggestion of Death*

"A wonderful, twisted tour through legal education that had me laughing all the way. ... [T]he perfect antidote for legal education ... [A] must read for law students, professors and lawyers."

— Professor Gerry Hess, Director of the Institute for Law School Teaching

"Hard to find words to describe it. Spectabulous? Fanacular? McClurg brings legal humor to new heights. ... Very, very funny!"

— Professor Myron Moskovitz, leading casebook and treatise author

"What a 'Trip'! Hilariously poking fun at law students, professors, judges, and the law itself, Andrew McClurg's *The Law School Trip* is truly a classic of legal humor."

— Professor David G. Owen, leading tort law expert and author

"A delicious read from beginning to end."

— Grif Stockley, bestselling author of *Probable Cause* and *Religious Conviction*

[1]FOOTNOTE
PRESS

A Footnote Press book,
published in association with Trafford Publishing.

Cover art, illustrations and mixed drinks by Gary Wayne Golden.
www.garywaynegolden.com

TRAFFORD

This book was published on-demand
in cooperation with Trafford Publishing.

On-demand publishing is a unique process and service of making a book
available for retail sale to the public taking advantage of on-demand
manufacturing and Internet marketing. On-demand publishing includes
promotions, retail sales, manufacturing, order fulfilment, accounting and
collecting royalties on behalf of the author.

Suite 6E, 2333 Government St.
Victoria, B.C. V8T 4P4, CANADA
Phone: 250-383-6864   Fax: 250-383-6804
Toll-free: 1-888-232-4444 (Canada & US)
E-mail: sales@trafford.com   Web site: www.trafford.com
Trafford Publishing is a division of Trafford Holdings Ltd.
Trafford Catalogue #01-0048
www.trafford.com/robots/01-0048.html

10   9   8   7   6   5   4   3

National Library of Canada Cataloguing in Publication Data

McClurg, Andrew J., 1954-
The law school trip

ISBN 1-55212-646-3

1. Law schools—Humor. 2. Law students—Humor.
I. Title. II. Title: Insider's guide to law school.
PN6231.L4M32 2001   340'.071'1   C2001-910349-2

THE INSIDER'S GUIDE
TO LAW SCHOOL

Andrew J. McClurg

Designed and Illustrated by Gary Wayne Golden

[1]FOOTNOTE
PRESS

For Kody and Caitlin

Preface

This book parodies just about everyone and everything connected to legal education, including myself, but it's just for fun. Don't take anything in here too seriously. While this book contains many insights about law school, much of it is just the product of my twisted brain.

Law school is a great place to be. In teaching at law schools in Arkansas, California, Colorado, Florida, and North Carolina, I've found one dominant consistency: the nation's law schools are exciting learning environments brimming with bright, hard-working and ethical students taught by distinguished professionals. Legal education is in fine shape, and I feel fortunate to be a part of it.

Portions of this book originally appeared in my *Harmless Error* column in the *American Bar Association Journal*, usually in a modified form. "The Recommendation Letter," also slightly modified, first appeared in the *Journal of Legal Education*.

I have some thanks to give. Several friends read drafts of this book and offered suggestions that made it better, including Coleen Barger, Heather Callaway, Lara Nather, Mary Pat Treuthart, and Debby Vickers. Lisa Broadwater generously (in more ways than one) applied her nonpareil editing skills to what I foolishly believed was a finished product. I am grateful and humbled that some very distinguished lawyers, law professors and authors—including Jacquie Brennan, Charles Crawford, Mark Drumbl, Gerry Hess, Myron Moskovitz, David Owen, Grif Stockley, Marianne Wesson, and Tim Zinnecker—have been willing to say nice things about this book and actually put them in writing. The groovy cover and cool page layout are products of the incredibly creative brain of digital artist Gary Wayne Golden. Gary's going to be famous someday, and I'll be able to say he worked on *The Law School Trip*.

Special thanks to all of my current and former law students. Their dedication, intelligence and effervescent spirit make teaching law the best job in the world and keep me optimistic about the future of the legal profession. Above all else, this book is a tribute to the weird and wonderful experience we force them to endure to earn the title of "lawyer."

My daughter, Caitlin, is the inspiration not only for Suzy Spikes, but for just about everything. Finally, I thank Kody Linn Logan, who gave me more than I could ever repay even if I had the chance. We all still miss you every day, Kody.

— Andrew J. McClurg

TABLE OF CONTENTS

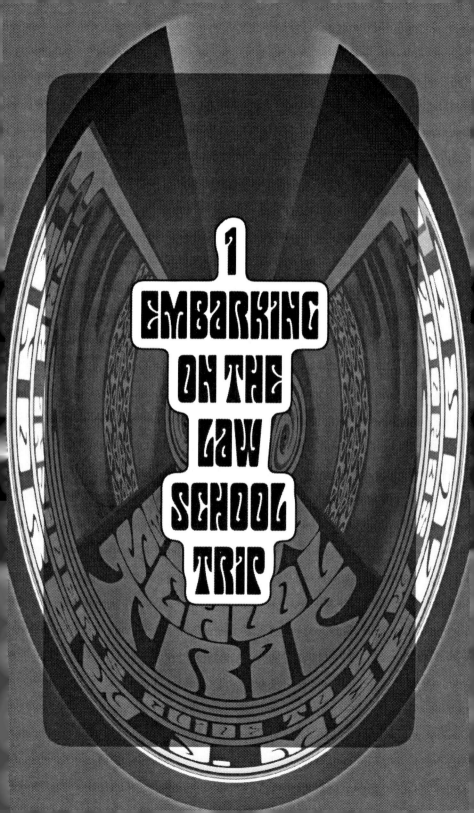

1

EMBARKING ON THE LAW SCHOOL TRIP

Welcome to *The Law School Trip*, the authoritative insider's guide to law school.[1] If you are reading these words, you must be either considering law school (bully for you!), attending law school (go set the world on fire!) or practicing law (so sorry). Whichever your situation, this book is for you. Never before have so many mysteries of legal education been illuminated in so few pages in so many fonts.

Why is this book called *The Law School Trip*? Because attending law school and ingesting lysergic acid diethylamide, or LSD, have been scientifically proven to produce nearly identical effects in the human brain.

Both are mind-blowing experiences. Both alter one's perception of reality. Both can be understood only by those who actually experience them. And both present grave dangers of severe adverse reactions. Studies show the main difference is that law school costs more. According to a well-known guide to law school on reserve in our law

---

[1] Hi. How's it going? How about those _____ (insert favorite sports team)? They really are (something special/fun to watch/an embarrassment to the community). Do you think they have a chance to (make the playoffs/go all the way/avoid major felony convictions) this season?

I'm trying to ease you gently into the world of legal footnoting. You need to know up front that the law loves footnotes. If the law could have romantic relations, it would be with a footnote. It wouldn't be pretty, but a lot of things in law aren't. You'll see more footnotes your first week of law school than in your entire life. Law professors and

library, tuition at elite private schools now costs more than $28,000 per year, whereas according to a well-known drug dealer on reserve in our state correctional facility, a dose of LSD costs only about five bucks.

PRODUCT WARNING: AUTHOR HAS NEVER TAKEN LSD AND DOES NOT RECOMMEND IT, EXCEPT PERHAPS DURING CIVIL PROCEDURE EXAM.

There are numerous examples of this mind-blowing, reality-altering, adverse-reaction-inducing phenomenon, many of which are discussed in this book. Here's one to start you out. Your professors are going to pose endless questions to you. At the beginning of law school, you will naively think these questions have simple answers. Indeed, if they were posed in the outside world, they would. Unfortunately, once a question is designated as a "legal question," the possible answers to it expand to infinity.

To understand this phenomenon, imagine you just dropped acid and are trying to decide whether to go to the

---

judges even write articles about footnotes. No joke. Check these out: *In Praise of Footnotes*, 167 Federal Rules Decisions 283 (1996); *A Footnote to a Footnote*, 75 Michigan Bar Journal 494 (1996); *In Defense of Footnotes*, National Law Journal, June 20, 1988, at 13.

I could go on and on about footnotes—and should—because that's the purpose of legal footnotes: to provide a loophole to the fundamental rule of good writing that you should stop when you get to the end of a sentence. Footnotes allow a thought to continue indefinitely. I confess that I love footnotes. Like many law professors, I feel safer and more secure in a footnote than in the wide open, often terrifying, world of text. If it were up to me, I'd finish the entire book in this footnote.

convenience store to get some milk. Normally, this would be a simple choice between two options: (1) I will go to the convenience store to get some milk; or (2) I will not go to the convenience store to get some milk. But the consciousness-expanding effects of LSD enlarge the choices dramatically:

- I will go to the store to get some milk, but first I will wait until the sky is no longer purple.

- I will not go to the convenience store to get some milk. I will stay home and milk my cat instead.

- I will go to the convenience store, but instead of buying milk I will shoplift a can of tomato juice. When I get to prison, I will ask for milk.

- I will go to the convenience store to get some milk, but will forget why I went there, so I will turn around and head back home, but I will forget where my home is and drive to Mercury where I will buy some milk.

- I will go to the convenience store and buy a Slim Jim and use alchemy to change it into milk, or if not milk, gold, in which case I will use the gold to buy a milk factory so I will never have to go to the convenience store to buy milk.

Legal analysis works in the same fashion. There is no such thing as a simple or concrete answer to a legal question.

Studies show the most accurate answer to most legal questions is: "Beats the heck out of me." The indefinite nature of the law is one of the most frustrating and perplexing aspects of life for new law students. You'll spend every waking moment learning thousands of complex legal rules only to be told in class they don't provide right answers, just good arguments. Then you'll take your first law school exams and learn that there really are right answers, because you got everything wrong. Don't try to make sense of it. You can't do it. Just accept that you've embarked on the law school trip.

Before I let you in on any other secrets of legal education, I need to take care of a dicey legal matter.

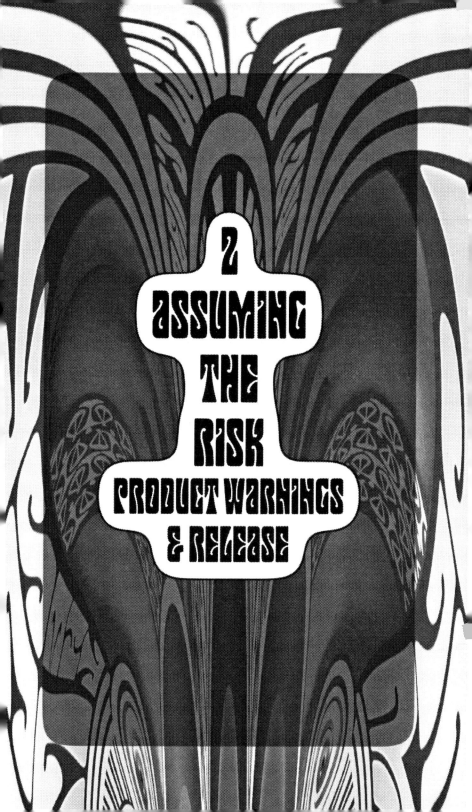

2
ASSUMING THE RISK
PRODUCT WARNINGS & RELEASE

ne of the first things you will learn in law school is that, in America, you can get sued at the drop of a hat, especially if the hat is made of asbestos or is small enough to pose a choking hazard to children. Like it or not, we live in a litigious society. Worried that a court might declare this book to be a defective product, the publisher has insisted that I give you, the legally-inclined reader, complete warnings concerning the many potential dangers of this product:

PRODUCT WARNINGS:
• FOR EXTERNAL USE. INTENDED FOR FIGURA-TIVE CONSUMPTION ONLY.
• STORE SAFELY WHEN NOT IN USE. NEVER LEAVE BOOK ON SHELF WHERE SPIDERS COULD TRIP OVER IT AND BREAK SEVERAL LEGS.
• PRODUCT MAY CAUSE USER TO CRAMP OVER TOILET VOMITING WITH LAUGHTER. TEQUILA SHOTS MAY ACCENTUATE THIS EFFECT. ON THE OTHER HAND, A COUPLE OF BEERS USUALLY CONTRIBUTE TO A MORE PLEASURABLE READ-ING EXPERIENCE.
• DO NOT READ IN DARK. JOKES FUNNIER WHEN VISIBLE.
• NEVER TAPE BOOK TO FACE WHILE OPERATING MOVING VEHICLE AS VISION WILL BE OBSCURED.

IF BOOK IS TAPED TO FACE WHILE DRIVING, PULL OVER IMMEDIATELY. REMOVE BOOK FROM FACE. ASK YOURSELF, "WHY WAS I DRIVING WITH A BOOK TAPED TO MY FACE?" IF YOU CANNOT THINK OF AN EXCELLENT ANSWER, DISCONTINUE USE AND CONSULT A QUALIFIED MENTAL HEALTH PROFESSIONAL.

• KEEP THIS AND ALL BOOKS OUT OF THE REACH OF CHILDREN AS THEY WILL INTERFERE WITH THEIR MTV.

• NOT INTENDED FOR USE AS FLOTATION DEVICE UNLESS EQUIPPED WITH OPTIONAL FLOTATION ACCESSORY (NOT AVAILABLE IN PAPERBACK).

• **PUBLISHER DOES NOT VOUCH FOR MCCLURG AND WILL CLAIM TO HAVE NEVER HEARD OF HIM IN THE EVENT OF TROUBLE.**

Additional product warnings are posted throughout the book. Unfortunately, there simply is not enough space to include all necessary warnings. Readers are urged to consult the full product warnings for this book contained in the companion volume, *Product Warnings for the Law School Trip.* The product warnings for that volume are available in *Product Warnings to the Product Warnings for the Law School Trip.*

PRODUCT WARNING: BEFORE USING PRODUCT, READ AND FOLLOW ALL WARNINGS AND WARNINGS TO WARNINGS, INCLUDING THIS WARNING WARNING YOU TO READ AND FOLLOW ALL WARNINGS AND WARNINGS TO WARNINGS.

Just to be on the safe side, before proceeding further, please sign the release form below:

RELEASE OF ALL CLAIMS

CAUTION: Do NOT Read Before Signing

The undersigned, his/her heirs, agents, servants, employees, executors, representatives, successors, assigns, friends, pets, lovers, ex-spouses, and personal trainers, do for valuable consideration, including, but not limited to, smiles, chuckles, giggles, chortles, cackles, belly-laughs, guffaws, roars, shrieks, snorts and screeches, hereby release, acquit and forever discharge Author and Publisher of any and all claims, demands, causes of action, loss, damages, injuries, attorneys' fees, jail sentences, parking tickets and costs of any kind growing out of, related to, or arising from the use of *The Law School Trip (the insider's guide to law school)* for the purpose of reading, perusing, skimming, plagiarizing, door-propping, roach-swatting, hamster-cage-lining, corporal-punishment inflicting, or any other purpose.

Buyer: _____

Witness: _____

Witness: _____

Witness: _____

Witness: _____

Witness: _____

Witness: _____

Enjoy *The Law School Trip,* but don't say I didn't warn you.

3

GETTING STARTED

efore deciding to take the law school trip, you have many things to consider. Your life is about to change completely and irrevocably. Leisure time will become a quaint notion of the past. "Amortization" will become the most important word in your vocabulary as you watch your student loans surpass the debt of several Latin American countries and even some American credit card holders. You will suddenly become the most boring person in the world to your family and friends as you regale them with fascinating details of 16th-century cases from the Court of Assizes. Worst of all, because the primary goal of law school is to teach you to "think like a lawyer," you will never again enjoy the luxury of thinking like an unemployed undergraduate student. With so much at stake, pause and step back. Reflect on some of the fine points of the decision-making process that many applicants overlook, beginning with:

Why Do You Want to be a Lawyer?

Before applying to law school, it's important to understand why you want to be a lawyer. You need to know the answer to this question so you can decide whether you possess the will to survive a suffocating workload for three grueling years, so you can evaluate whether you have the mental toughness necessary to

succeed and so you can take stock of your commitment to social justice. But mostly you need to know the answer because "Why do you want to be a lawyer?" is the question most asked by law professors upon meeting new students.[2]

Since it's important to make a good first impression on your professors, take the time to compose and memorize a good answer to the question, remembering that law schools are the nation's bastions of elite political correctness:

Great Answer:
I want to be a lawyer so I can lead America into a new millennium of liberalism, globalism, multi-culturalism, transgenderism, just about anything I can stick an *ism* on. I will embrace all people, regardless of race, creed, or number of failed relationships. However, I will only embrace them figuratively because I am steadfastly against sexual harassment in any form. When not busy studying or recycling my class notes, I will prove my commitment to tolerance by resisting the urge to kill people who talk on cell phones in restaurants.

Average Answer:
I want a challenging and rewarding career.

Poor Answer:
I want to get rich and not work very hard.

---

[2] The second most-asked question is: "Do you have any idea how brilliant we are?"

Bad Answer:
I want to sue doctors' asses off.

Terrible Answer:
I want to squash the little guy.

Who Goes to Law School?

Who goes to law school? Everyone. On the first day, you'll run into old friends, ex-spouses, long-lost relatives, missing Korean War veterans and Jimmy Hoffa. The U.S. has more than 900,000 lawyers, 130,000 law students and 100,000 law school applicants each year. Law school deans are expecting these numbers to rise in light of surveys showing that 99 percent of all Americans "think about" going to law school.

In 1951 the ratio of U.S. lawyers to population was 1 to 695. By 2000, that ratio declined to 1 to 267. According to the U.S. Census Bureau, the standard two-parent household was recently surpassed by the five-lawyer household. Just last week, my neighbors changed the name on their mailbox from "The Snurds" to "Snurd, Snurd, Snurd, Snurd & Snurd, Limited Liability Partnership." The U.S. has far more lawyers per capita than any other country. Why the large discrepancy? Experts attribute it to cultural differences, primarily the fact that in our culture we like to sue each other a lot and in other cultures they don't.

Another reason for so many lawyers in the U.S. is that law school is the only professional degree program with no course prerequisites. All other professional degrees require

prior planning. Doctors, accountants, dentists, veterinarians—they all have to complete long lists of required courses before enrolling in their professional programs.

But thank a gender-neutral, non-denominational higher power for the Juris Doctor degree. A four-year degree in any discipline suffices as an apprenticeship to the law: music, philosophy, ballroom dancing, sheet metal work, it doesn't matter. This is good news for law schools. So long as the continued pursuit of higher education remains our nation's and our parents' only socially-approved excuse for not getting a life, law schools are guaranteed a steady stream of applicants. It's also good news for applicants who worked four years to get an undergraduate degree that qualifies them to do nothing but seek a graduate degree. Wondering what to do with your degree in Medieval Studies of What Happened on the Afternoon of April 12, 1257? Don't feel quite prepared for the real world? No problem. Apply to law school. Everyone does eventually.

Skin Thickening

Being a lawyer is tough, and I'm not talking just about the high stress and long hours. It's a challenge simply surviving day to day in a world where sizable groups of people purport to "hate lawyers." True story: I recently went on a canoeing trip with a group of law professors. The woman at the canoe rental place asked what I did and I said, "Law professor." Without hesitating, she said, "I hate lawyers." Without hesitating, I replied, "I hate people who rent

canoes." She was shocked and appalled that I would say something so rude. Although the irony was lost on her, I felt good about standing up for my profession; plus, I really do hate people who rent canoes.

Before finally deciding on law school, make sure you have very thick skin. Perform this test: Plunge a needle into a chicken breast. Plunge a needle into your own breast. (Not the same needle. Never share needles with a chicken. Many modern fowl are intravenous hormone users.) Measure your relative skin thickness by whether the chicken is able to peck your eyes out before you dial 911. Kidding. Use a frozen chicken breast. Still kidding. I'm really talking about EMOTIONAL skin thickness.

If it hurts your feelings when people treat you like fecal matter, do not become a lawyer. You are entering the only profession where strangers feel free, compelled even, to insult you to your face. Be prepared for every person you meet to tell you offensive jokes and explain how much they detest your chosen lifelong pursuit.

No other workers in America get such rude treatment, certainly not to their face. People don't make fun of accountants for having the most boring job in the world, berate convenience store clerks for being losers or kid doctors about malpractice lawsuits. But upon meeting a lawyer every trace of etiquette and common courtesy vanishes. Here's an oft-repeated cocktail party scene:

Lawyer: Hi, I'm Fred.

Stranger: What do you do, Fred?

Lawyer: I'm a lawyer.

Stranger: I hate your guts, Fred. I want to kill you.

Lawyer: Um… I think I'll get a drink.

Stranger: Fred, you alcoholic, ambulance-chasing scum—don't you dare walk away until I've told you at least forty of my favorite lawyer jokes. Three lawyers are sitting in a bar with a cockroach, Charles Manson and the devil…

Lawyer: Thanks, I've already heard it.

Stranger: Figures. Arrogant too.

Before setting foot in a law school, prepare yourself to be constantly judged and criticized. If you need help training, call someone's mom.

Choosing a Law School

If you're still reading, you must have made up your mind to be a lawyer. Perhaps you even like the idea of being verbally abused by strangers. Maybe you're shy and see it as a good way to meet people. The next important question to focus on is: Where should I go to law school? There are more than 180 law schools accredited by the American Bar Association, a few others seeking accreditation and a

bunch of unaccredited ones. How do you decide which law school is best for you?

First, be realistic. The choice may not be as hard as it appears. If you graduated with an 0-point from Yanni & Enya's University Without Walls with a degree in Breathing and get a card from the LSAT® examiners thanking you for the laughs, don't waste your time applying to a top school.

An exception to this rule is if you are disadvantaged in some way. Make no mistake. I'm not talking about real disadvantages, which are valid and important factors to consider in making admissions decisions. I'm talking about disadvantages that exist only for purposes of applying to law school. Everyone has been disadvantaged in some way. There's no reason you should be left out. These are some random samples of severe disadvantageousness drawn from law school application letters:

"I dress like a dork."

"Someone hurt my feelings once."

"My cat died tragically."

In asserting your disadvantage, take an aggressive approach. Here is an actual fake letter that got a student admitted to a top-ranked law school:

RE: *Your* request for additional information about my *application*

I am shocked and appalled that you have **the** nerve to ask me **to** justify my existence to you. I should and probably will sue you for Wasting *my* time. **My** doctor says you are *legally* required to admit me because **I** suffer from a severe disability:

I AM A COMPLETE JERK.

P.S. Your catalog said you value diversity. I am one of only a **small** number of American cans with a personal stockpile of mustard gas.

A weekly news magazine, *U.S. News & World Report*, publishes an annual ranking of all law schools. An amazingly high percentage of law students rely on these rankings in deciding where to apply and attend law school. However, a school's *U.S. News* ranking has little to do with the quality of education a student can expect to receive there. I have taught at four law schools, two of them ranked in the current top tier and two ranked in lower tiers. In terms of the core legal education received by the students, all four schools seemed about the same—really good.

One of the problems with the *U.S. News* rankings is their inclusion of a law school's "reputation" as a ranking criterion. Like people, some schools have better reputations than others. And like people, these reputations—good and bad—are not always warranted. A few years ago, I served as chair of my former law school's faculty recruitment committee. In this capacity, I received a letter from *U.S. News* asking me to rank the reputation of all of the nation's accredited law schools—approximately 175 schools at that time—from best to worst. I felt ridiculous trying to decide, with no basis in personal knowledge, whether Harvard is better than Yale or the University of Pittsburgh is better than the University of Idaho, or even whether Harvard is better than the University of Idaho. How could anyone know without attending or teaching at each school?

It has been reported that one critic of the rankings sent out her own law school ranking survey, which included the Massachusetts Institute of Technology and Penn State University. Both of these fine universities fared well in the

rankings, which is not surprising except for the fact that *they didn't have law schools.*[3]

In 1998, the deans of 150 law schools sent a letter to *U.S. News*, stating: "We hope to convince you to abandon an enterprise which we believe you should regard as an embarrassment to your magazine." The magazine declined to abandon the rankings, although it did make some adjustments in the process. Today, the rankings are more powerful and popular than ever.

The biggest problem with the *U.S. News* rankings is that they ignore the factors most important to the quality of a law student's life. So forget the *U.S. News* rankings. Use McClurg's Law Student Happiness rankings, which ranks schools according to the three things that matter most to student happiness: cost, location and whether the school hires entertaining professors. The McClurg formula changes the rankings dramatically as seen in this example:

Unnamed Famous Law School

U.S. News **rank:**	Top 10.
Student happiness rank:	174.
Tuition:	$28,000 per year and rising.
Location:	Somewhere snowy, way up north.
Faculty:	Professors at this school have served as Cabinet members, Congresspersons

---

[3] Penn State University subsequently absorbed Dickinson, a private independent law school, in 1997.

and Supreme Court justices. They have published millions of footnotes in distinguished law reviews.

Waukaloa Law School and Jet-Ski Rentals

U.S. News rank: Unranked.
Student happiness rank: Two righteous thumbs up.
Tuition: $3,000 per year, plus water sports activity fee.
Location: Sunny beach.
Faculty: Professors at this law school have served as comedians, magicians and rock stars. They have told millions of jokes in distinguished nightclubs.

The most important question you need to ask yourself in selecting a law school is "Will I be happy there?" The answer is "probably not," so it doesn't really matter which school you choose.

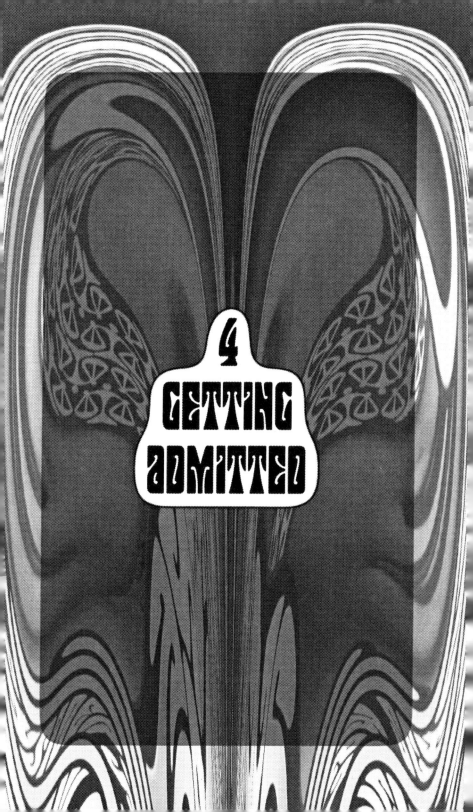

4
GETTING ADMITTED

aw schools weigh several factors in making the decision whether to admit an applicant, including your LSAT® score, undergraduate transcript, "personal statement," letters of reference, and market forces.

The LSAT®

All ABA-accredited and many non-accredited law schools require applicants to take the Law School Admission Test, or LSAT®. The LSAT® is designed to be a predictive indicator of how well a person will do in law school. Your LSAT® score is probably the most critical factor in determining whether you get admitted to the law school of your choice. The good news is that there are lots of preparatory materials available to help you get ready for it. For example, the Law School Admissions Council, Inc.— the good folks behind the LSAT®—publishes:

The Official LSAT PrepTest®
LSAT: The Official TriplePrep®
LSAT: The Offical TriplePrep Plus with Explanations®
and
L®S®A®T®: The Official® QuadraPrep®
PremiumUltraPlus® with Explanations® Why You Should
Plan On Taking the L®S®A®T® Several Times®[4]

---

[4] The first three are real, but I made the last one up.

At this point, you may be asking yourself, "What's up with all the little ®s? Are those really necessary?" Yes. The use of registered trademark symbols is absolutely critical to staying out of legal trouble for trademark infringement. In modern times, intellectual property lawyers have become the pitbulls of the legal profession, making O.J.'s Dream Team seem like a bunch of wimps in comparison. The Walt Disney Company, well-known for its aggressive enforcement of its intellectual property rights, once threatened to sue a Florida daycare center for painting unauthorized pictures of Disney characters on the wall.

But back to the LSAT®. The LSAT® contains three sections, designed to test reading comprehension, analytical reasoning and logical reasoning. A fourth section used to test purely illogical emotions, but was deleted after several test takers reported being disturbed during the exam by other test takers forming relationships, breaking them off and getting back together again.

Since analytical reasoning is the key ingredient to thinking like a lawyer, we'll focus on that section. The analytical reasoning section is designed to measure a person's ability to understand relational structures among things, events and people. Unfortunately, the questions in this section are incredibly HARD. In reviewing old LSAT® tests while writing this chapter, I was amazed I ever got a single question correct. Here are some sample questions:

LSAT® Sample Questions: Analytical Reasoning

Instructions. The following questions are based on a set of conditions. Carefully select your answer, then close your eyes and randomly blacken a space on the score sheet. Good luck! Ha, ha.

Question 1. Analyze the relationship structure among the following dots. Place them in order from most important to least important:

Questions 2-6. Assume that exactly six of the dots are representatives at a national punctuation conference. Six chairs are evenly spaced around a table. The chairs are numbered 1 through 6, with successively numbered chairs next to each other and chair number 1 next to chair number 6. Each chair is occupied by one of the dots. The following conditions apply:
    . must sit immediately next to .
    . must sit immediately next to ., ., or both
    . can sit anywhere except in front of the coat rack in the corner because it makes him look like ! and he is already sensitive about his reputation for

having a shrill temperament

., ., or . must be seated at the end of this sentence, so that it is grammatically correct.

2. Which of the following seating arrangements would NOT violate the stated conditions?
   (A) . . . . . .
   (B) . . . . . .
   (C) . . . . . .
   (D) . . . . . .
   (E) . . . . . .

3. Assume that . sits next to ., . sits next to ., . sits next to . and . sits next to . Assume further that their table is in the smoking section. Which of the following best describes the seating arrangement?
   (A) ??????
   (B) ??????
   (C) ??????
   (D) ??????
   (E) ??????

4. Assume each dot sits in its proper seat, except for ., who sits on ., with the resulting seating arrangement of . . : . . Which of the following is the most likely to result?
   (A) A violation of the stated conditions.
   (B) A game of musical chairs.
   (C) A broken pelvis.
   (D) A sexual harassment suit.

5. Assume the dots, feeling slighted as the only ones in the universe not asserting their intellectual property rights, hire an intellectual property lawyer to represent their interests. The lawyer will seat the dots in the following arrangement:

(A) .® .® .® .® .® .®

(B) .© .© .© .© .© .©

(C) .ᵀᴹ .ᵀᴹ .ᵀᴹ .ᵀᴹ .ᵀᴹ .ᵀᴹ

(D) .com .com .com .com .com .com

(E) All of the above.

6. Do you have a clue what any of this means? Indicate your answer through a proper structural relationship of the dots:

NO CLUE!

Undergraduate Transcript

Next to your LSAT® score, the most important factor in determining your admission is your undergraduate GPA®.[5] Evaluating undergraduate records poses a difficult challenge for admissions committees because undergraduate programs vary widely in their rigor.

Recently, a law school admissions committee was trying to decide between admitting one of two students. One student had an unimpressive undergraduate GPA of 2.4 on a 4.0

---

[5] Just kidding. GPA is not a registered trademark—yet.

scale, while the other had graduated with a perfect 4.0. Simple choice, you say. Not so fast. Review of the students' transcripts revealed subtle differences not apparent from the raw scores. It turned out the student with the 2.4 had graduated with a physics degree from MIT, where she took and passed courses such as *Advanced Human Cloning* and *Calculus XII* . On the other hand, the student with the perfect 4.0 graduated with a liberal arts degree from Brickyard University. His transcript looked like this:

CERTIFIED TRANSCRIPT

Course	Grade
Chaos Theory and Worldwide Wrestlingism	A
Beer Consumption in a Post-Industrial Society	A
Undergraduate Sleep Patterns (Lab)	A
Chutes and Ladders for Dummies	A
Technology Seminar: Introduction to Porn Sites	A

Fortunately for applicants who attended weaker under-graduate programs, some law schools use an "automatic admit" index system in which admission is based solely on a weighted mathematical computation of the applicant's LSAT® score and GPA. Transcripts might never be looked at unless the applicant's index score falls below the preset minimum score (which varies year to year depending on market forces—see below).

Falling below the automatic admit index score sends the applicant into the world of "discretionary admissions." Most schools set aside a certain number of seats (which can

vary year to year depending on market forces—see below) for discretionary admittees, students with lower LSAT® and GPA numbers who are nevertheless considered worthy candidates based on an evaluation of their overall application files. For these students, the next two items— the personal statement and reference letters—become vitally important.

Personal Statement

Most law schools require applicants to include a "personal statement" with their application. The purpose of the personal statement is to give applicants the opportunity to demonstrate that they have creative imaginations. Actually, the real purpose is to give applicants the opportunity to show they are interesting people with unique experiences and accomplishments that distinguish them from other applicants.[6]

However, many applicants make the mistake of misreading "personal statement" as "fictional statement." Some people overinflate their backgrounds in an attempt to fit the "applicant profile" they believe law school admissions committees are in search of: diverse candidates with a commitment to public service. Do not give in to this temptation. It's true that law schools, for good reasons, are interested in adding diversity to their classes by admitting persons who have overcome obstacles in life. Moreover, they justifiably look with favor on applicants with a

---

[6] Note that if your LSAT® and undergraduate GPA are high enough to qualify you for automatic admission, the chances are good that no one will ever read your personal statement, so you can write whatever you want.

demonstrated commitment to public service. But most people simply don't fit into these categories. Do not try to pass yourself off as Nelson Mandela or Mother Teresa.[7] Here's what can result when you try:

Personal Statement of Brandi Uppercrust

I have endured many struggles and hardships in my young life … only faith and perseverance allow me to carry on … one summer when I was only a teenager, I was forced to work an entire afternoon at The Gap® … involved in a tragic auto accident on my sixteenth birthday in which I broke a nail while untying the bow on the BMW Daddy gave me … my college years were filled with pain, as I endured the scorn of my sorority sisters due to a genetic condition over which I have no control: my amazing beauty … work long hours each week maintaining an even tan and ripped abs … emotionally scarred from the night I stood in front of the mirror and faced the harsh truth that I will not always be perfect …

I want to go to law school so I can help people. I am a kind, caring person who believes it is important to give back to the community … once gave a dollar to a homeless man who wouldn't stop hassling me … started Jaegermeister® bottle recycling program at my sorority … while studying in

---

[7] One applicant had the gall to actually sign her application "Mother Teresa." Several schools rejected her, much to their chagrin when she turned out to be the real Mother Teresa. Remember, everyone goes to law school.

Mexico, I often felt bad about the filthy little street urchins selling Chiclets® … benefit the needy by selling my clothes on consignment at a HUGE discount … only person in my sorority with the integrity and character to tell my roommate, Kelli, that Brittani, Tammi, Lindsi and Eleanori substituted Tic-Tacs® for her birth control pills ….

P.S. As you can see from the many registered trademark symbols I used, I have an excellent aptitude for intellectual property law, which I would use only to further humanity by threatening to sue daycare centers on behalf of giant corporations.

Just be yourself, for better or worse.

Reference Letters

Law schools require applicants to submit letters of reference in support of their applications. Unfortunately, many letters of recommendation come across as completely bogus. After years of study, linguists have determined the reason for this: they are completely bogus. Too often, students make the mistake of opting for "big names"—judges, politicians, lawyers—to write their reference letters rather than people who actually know them. As a result, law school admissions committees are flooded with letters that come across as something less than sincere, such as this letter written by a prominent U.S. Senator on behalf of applicant Daryl Langdon:

BERNARD SCHLEPCLOTT
UNITED STATES SENATOR

United States Senate
Washington, D. C.

January 26, 2001

Dear Admissions Committee:

It is my great pleasure to recommend Dernyl Plankton for admission to your law school. I feel I am well-qualified to comment on Durgle's qualifications because, although I've never actually met the young man, a generous contributor to my campaign who is a friend of Darnell's family showed me his college yearbook picture.

From my intimate acquaintance with this grainy black and white photograph, I can state confidently that Dino possesses all of the qualities necessary to do well in law school, including two more or less normally-placed eyes, relatively few acne scars and a sizable forehead, suggesting the presence of a decent-sized brain. Please admit Daphne to your law school, so my campaign contributor will quit harassing me.

Sincerely,

Bernard Schlepclott [8]

Bernard Schlepclott

---

[8] Signature written by machine.

Because law professors tend to be anti-authoritarian by nature, letters from muckety-mucks can have the opposite effect of what is intended. You are much better off getting a letter—preferably a favorable one—from a former teacher or employer who knows your capabilities.

Market Forces

Students are unaware of the large role market forces play in determining admissions to law school. The ease with which one can get admitted to law school depends on whether law school is "hot" or "cold" in the particular year you apply. Applications to the nation's law schools fluctuate wildly, usually in direct correlation to the number of lawyer shows on television. One year there might be a thousand applications for every available seat and the next year five total. For applicants, this means it's easier to get into law school some years than others, particularly at lower-ranked, tuition-driven private institutions.

This secret law school memorandum shows how the applicant pool can benefit from declining applications:

CONFIDENTIAL MEMORANDUM

To: All faculty
From: Your Dean
Re: Adjustment to Admissions Standards

You are all aware of the precipitous drop in our applications this year. As you also know, the success of our fine institution depends on us finding large numbers of people willing to pay us enormous sums of tuition. Thus, it is important that we maintain a healthy enrollment.

On the other hand, as your dean, it is my responsibility to ensure we maintain our high academic standards, tradition of excellence and the integrity of our admissions process.

Balancing these concerns, I am implementing a slight adjustment to our admissions criteria:

Old Standard: Any person of good moral character with a minimum Grade Point Average of 3.25 from an accredited undergraduate institution and who scored above the 75th percentile on the LSAT may be granted admission as an entering student.

New Standard: Any person with a checkbook who has not been declared legally brain-dead by a licensed medical examiner and is not serving hard time (unless eligible for parole before Fall Orientation) may be granted admission as an entering student.

Let's proceed on the assumption everything goes well for you. You fare well on the LSAT®, manage to escape undergraduate school with a decent grade point average and get accepted to the law school of your choice. Now you can just sit back and relax, realizing that this will be your last chance to do so for the rest of your life.

5 THE FIRST DAYS

The first days of law school. Who can forget them? Palpitating heart, sweaty palms, waves of anxiety— and that's just trying to find a parking place. The first days of law school are unlike anything anyone has experienced, except for a few nontraditional students old enough to have survived Omaha Beach. You can feel the electricity in the air as you walk down the hall. Avoid it. It comes from high-voltage stun guns used to motivate third-year students.

Excited about actually starting law school? Great! Then let's go. On your mark, get ready, get set ... HOLD IT!

Dis-Orientation

Before you get to start learning the law, you have to go through Orientation. Although the specifics vary from school to school, Orientation is generally a week-long affair where professors and upper-level students attempt to "demystify" law school for new students. First, the new students meet with faculty members, who attempt to imprint upon them the importance of things like conscientious study techniques and diligent brief writing. Then they meet with upper-level students, who contradict every word the professors just said.

Whereas the advice given by professors always involves

ways to do more work, the advice given by other students always involves ways to do less work. A professor will say, "Study, study, study!," to which a 3L will retort, "Party, party, party!" Professors will sagely advise you to carefully brief every assigned case. Upper-level students will scoff and tell you to buy canned briefs, or even better, a used book where someone else has already "book-briefed" the cases in the margin.

Few activities are more fulfilling to 2Ls and 3Ls than giving advice to new students. If they are able to combine advice-giving with beer-drinking, something close to nirvana is achieved. This is one reason the number of first-semester parties sponsored by the student government and legal fraternities exceeds actual classroom hours.

Because students are so jazzed up about starting real classes, they often view Orientation as a waste of time, even though it provides a great deal of useful information. It's a very similar phenomenon to buying a new toy, such as a chain saw. When you get home and open the box, the last thing you want to do is spend three days studying the instruction manual and lengthy product warnings. You want to pour some gas in the sucker, crank it up and drive quickly to the hospital to get your thigh sewed back on.

Since planning for and applying to law school usually involves a long-term process in which students have already done a considerable amount of waiting, it's understandable they are disappointed to learn on arrival that they first have to undergo a lengthy orientation process. A student once analogized Orientation to having sex for the first time:

You've waited all your life. You've dreamed about it, planned for it, simulated it and now the day finally arrives that you get to actually DO IT. You're totally psyched, when all of a sudden a bunch of people burst into the room and say, "STOP! YOU CANNOT HAVE SEX RIGHT NOW. BEFORE YOU CAN HAVE SEX, YOU MUST SIT DOWN AND LISTEN TO US TELL YOU FOR AN ENTIRE WEEK WHAT IT IS *LIKE* TO HAVE SEX."

Many students miss the value of Orientation because they are chomping at the bit to get started. They can only concentrate on the ...

First Day of Classes

When you enter a law school classroom for the first time, you'll step into a bubbling cauldron of excitement, confusion and primal terror. A tornado of questions overwhelm students on that unforgettable first day of classes:

1. **Am I well-prepared enough?**
2. **Can I really do this?**
3. **Is everyone here brilliant except me?**
4. **Is there really such thing as "justice" in the universe?**
5. **How do I look?**
6. **What's this on the used casebook I bought? Blood?**

7. Will I achieve my lifelong dream of becoming
   … wait a second …
8. What time does this class end?
9. Is that clock right?
10. Is that clock right?

But, of course, the dominant question on the minds of law students the first day is: AM I GOING TO GET CALLED ON? This question haunts students throughout all of law school and—for that small but statistically significant percentage of students who end up institutionalized—24 hours a day forever.

The Socratic Method

All this anxiety is attributable to the Socratic method. Law professors love the Socratic method. We hated it in law school, but now we've come to appreciate the great usefulness of probing questions as a dialectical tool for unearthing new knowledge. Besides, it's fun scaring the hell out of people.

In the interest of fairness, here are the two competing definitions of the Socratic method …

Law Professor's Definition: "The Socratic Method is the sword of knowledge. Through incisive questioning, I am able to hurl the student down the path of wisdom to the mother lode of insight."

Law Student's Definition: "All the freakin' guy ever does is ask questions. He hasn't answered one all year. I'm clueless."

Students often perceive the Socratic method as a kind of unfair mind-reading game, which is understandable since professors frequently ask questions like, "Mr. Smith, what am I thinking about this case?" The Socratic method is unique to legal education. Medical schools don't use it, which, in addition to getting to walk around in a white coat saying "I'm the doctor," is a good reason to go to medical school instead of law school. You would never hear a medical school professor ask, "Mr. Smith, what am I thinking about this pancreas?" She would just tell you, then send you a large bill.

Socratic Simulation Exercise

To prepare yourself for the Socratic method, practice with this simulation exercise.

Instructions: First, put yourself in a mental and physical state that approximates getting called on in front of 100 competitive rivals and being expected to say something brilliant about something you've never thought about before.

Spin in rapid circles. When you reach 100 rpms, pump one gallon of fast-acting laxative down your esophagus using a pressure sprayer of not less than 12 hp. Strip naked and chain your neck to the side of a steaming radiator. Smash yourself in the temple three times with a ball-peen hammer. Load a revolver with one cartridge. Spin the cylinder. Place gun to head. Pull the trigger as you analyze the following question:

A shoots at B, but misses and hits C, who loses control of her car and crashes into D, driving a school bus full of children (H, I, J, K, L, M, N, O and P) down a winding mountain road. The school bus careens into a gas pump at the exact second lightning hits the pump. In the explosion, a piece of glass, E, hits F, walking his dog, G, nearby. G gets loose, tries briefly to mate with Q, then viciously attacks R as he carries an armload of law books up a staircase. The books fall on T, causing massive head injuries. T is rushed to the ER by EMTs, gets CPR from an RN and an IV from an MD, but it's too late. He's DOA. To make matters worse, his HMO refuses to pay for his MRI. What color is the school bus?

You have approximately 10 seconds to answer before your classmates begin shifting in their seats. This occurs for three reasons: (1) Most of your classmates feel sorry for you but are trying to look engrossed in their notes so they don't get called on in the likelihood you are unable to answer the question correctly; (2) One student—the same one every time—started waving his arm frantically the instant the professor opened her mouth; (3) A few, who will go on to become intellectual property lawyers, are leaning forward to get a closer view of your suffering.[9]

---

[9] I don't really have anything against intellectual property lawyers, but I do feel strongly that the overly-aggressive assertion

Making Friends

A good strategy for coping with any strange environment is to make a friend, and law school is no exception. Fortunately, making friends in law school is easy because of the psychological bonding effect of group terror.

In one famous social psychology experiment, researchers put a group of monkeys in the same cage with a group of lions. Monkeys and lions usually don't socialize because the lions eat the monkeys, which causes hard feelings. Early in the experiment, it appeared events would follow this customary pattern as the lions began chasing the monkeys and the monkeys began bonking the lions on the heads with coconuts.

At this point, the researchers inserted a Contracts professor into the cage who began conducting a Socratic dialogue about the doctrine of promissory estoppel. An amazing transformation occurred. The lions and monkeys immediately locked paws and began singing drinking songs. Within a few minutes, the lions were giving the monkeys foot massages and the monkeys were encouraging the lions to get in touch with their inner cubs.

PRODUCT WARNING: DO NOT PUT CONTRACTS PROFESSORS IN CAGES WITH WILD ANIMALS. AUTHOR NOT RESPONSIBLE FOR TOOTH OR CLAW WOUNDS TO CONTRACTS PROFESSORS.

---

of intellectual property rights threatens free speech and open communication. You can quote me on that. However, if you do it without written permission, you'll be hearing from my intellectual property lawyer.

Mutual panic brings people, and wild animals, together. Everyone is desperate for friendship and support on the first day of law school. All you have to do to become close friends with your seatmate is not kill him. He will be so grateful for this outward display of affection that you will be best pals for life and perhaps even marry.

Talking the Talk

One of the things that makes the first days of law school so scary is all the new terminology. The law has a language of its own, which can be intimidating until you get a handle on it. Sometimes it will sound like your professors are speaking a foreign language. One poor student passed out from fright on the first day because she couldn't understand a word the professor was saying. Only upon being revived did she learn he was a visiting professor from Pakistan.

The intimidation factor is increased by the fact that several of your classmates will have had some exposure to legalese and will toss it around with seeming aplomb. Often, these are students who have taken a couple of undergraduate law courses on their way to a degree in criminal justice or political science. These students brim with confidence over the fact that they know almost a half dozen things about the law. The fact that there are more than sixty trillion things they don't know does not deter them from aggressively demonstrating their knowledge.

To boost your legal vocabulary buy a copy of *Black's Law Dictionary* and keep it nearby for handy reference. This classic reference work is a must-purchase for all law

students. I still consult my copy. Unfortunately, confusing legalese can often only be adequately defined by reference to other confusing legalese, so *Black's* doesn't always help.

For example, suppose you're diligently preparing for your first Property class and come across the popular property law term "enfeoff." This would occur in the context of someone "enfeoffing" someone else. Diligence and perhaps prurience should prompt you to pause and look the word up in *Black's*, which explains:

> **Enfeoff** — To invest with an estate by feoffment. To make a gift of any corporeal hereditaments to another. *See* Feoffment. [10]

Do you understand it now? No? Okay, then let's follow the instructions and "*See* Feoffment:"

> **Feoffment** — The gift of any corporeal hereditament to another, operating by transmutation of possession, and requiring, as essential to its completion, that the seisin be passed, which might be accomplished either by investiture or by livery of seisin. [11]

Still haven't quite got it? That's because you now also have to look up *corporeal, hereditament, transmutation, investiture, seisin* and *livery*. These definitions will in turn lead to dozens of other terms that need defining.

---

[10] BLACK'S LAW DICTIONARY 365 (6th ed. 1991)
[11] Id. at 429.

By the time you finish looking up "enfeoff" the first year will be over.

Briefing Cases

Most professors will tell you it is absolutely necessary to brief your cases, especially in the first year. A case brief is a capsule summary of a judicial opinion, including the pertinent facts, the holding of the court and the reasoning. New students, not knowing what's important in a case, have a hard time deciding what to include in their case briefs, so they include EVERYTHING. Early briefs are so long they often require an index and table of contents. However, this changes rapidly. By the end of the first year, briefs—for those still writing them—look more like this:

Case Brief for *NEW YORK TIMES v. SULLIVAN*
(U.S. 1964)
Defendant wins (I think).

The key to a good case brief is to identify the *narrow* legal issue involved in the case. New law students tend to view the issue much too broadly. To see what I'm talking about, let's compare examples of good (narrow) issue identification and bad (too broad) issue identification using the famous U.S. Supreme Court case of *Flast v. Cohen* (1968) as an example. *Flast* involved the constitutional doctrine known as "taxpayer standing":

Good Issue Identification

Issue: The issue in this case is whether a taxpayer has the power under Article III of the federal constitution to bring a lawsuit challenging a government spending decision.

Bad Issue Identification

Issue: The issue in this case has something to do with law.

How to Avoid Becoming the Object of Slanderous Rumors

One pitfall to beware of during the early weeks of law school is becoming the object of slanderous rumors. Law students talk about only two subjects: their classmates and their professors. Oh sure, once in a while a student will bring up actual law in a conversation, but she will be quickly drowned out by much more crucial topics such as whether a classmate does or does not qualify as a hottie.

Because law school is such a stultifying existence, students tend to embellish when relating colorful anecdotes about their colleagues and professors. The fact that a story is too fantastic to be believed only adds to the vigor with which it is spread. For example, if Professor Geeker passes Lila Kissup in the third-floor hallway and says "Hello," the story will be related by a witness as: "I saw Professor Geeker flirting with Lila Kissup in the third-floor hallway." This version will in turn be passed on as: "I heard Professor Geeker asked Lila Kissup out on a date in the

third-floor hallway."

It keeps going like this until the final version—the one with staying power that gets handed down for generations—is:

> **Omigawd, did you hear about Professor Geeker and Lila Kissup? They had sex right in the third-floor hallway! I can hardly believe it since Professor Geeker is a 92-year-old, blind, impotent, one-legged Shaker in a wheelchair. But since someone told me about it, I'm totally convinced it is a 100 percent true story.**

I almost forgot that I promised to tell you how to avoid becoming a victim of the law school rumor mill. The best method is to attend graduate school in psychology. You'll still be the victim of vicious rumors, but there will be more people around to help you deal with your emotional scars.

Take heart. You will survive the first days of law school. Your colon will be twisted like a garden hose and your ulcerated stomach could double as a colander, but you will survive.

6

LAW
FACULTY

aw professors are an unusual breed, which is a nice way of saying they're a bit quirky, which is a quaint way of saying they're weirdos, which is an unflattering way of saying they're total freakazoids.

We don't start out that way. Most new professors arrive at law schools as perfectly normal human beings, but this changes quickly because unlike the rest of the world, law professors aren't bound by normal workplace rules. In fact, there's a premium on eccentricity and obstinance. A lawyer who gets mad and tells her senior partner to insert his cell phone where the sun don't shine would be viewed as insubordinate and fired. However, a law professor who gets mad and tells her dean to insert his endowed chair in the same sunlight-deprived space would be admired as iconoclastic and perhaps receive a hefty raise. If she raises the idea at a faculty meeting, there's a good chance it will be adopted as official law school policy.

This evolution from normal human beings to oddball academics can be subtle. It's usually first detectable in minor lifestyle choices such as dress. There's the oft-repeated tale of the new law professor who arrives for the fall semester fresh from a big corporate law firm wearing navy blue suits, starched white shirts, silk rep ties and shiny wingtips. By the time Spring rolls around, he's walking around naked, head shaved, nipples

pierced, a tattoo of the great Judge Learned Hand covering his scalp, sticks of smoking incense emerging from various body orifices, and insisting he be called "The Professor Formerly Known as Ed."

Law students tend to hold their professors in awe, at least early on. Although this is flattering, it's also a bit embarrassing. Very few law professors are worthy of awe. We put our straitjackets on one leg at a time, just like everyone else. Being iconoclastic, most of us have tried it other ways—two legs at a time, an arm and a leg, a big toe and a baguette, over our heads, while playing a tuba—but, basically, we're just ordinary people.

Law professors are without exception extremely intelligent people. Many are brilliant. Unfortunately, a lot of this brilliance is wasted because law profs get no training on how to teach. To teach first-graders to spell "C-A-T" requires two years of undergraduate courses in education theory and practice. To teach complex legal analysis to adults requires only that one performed well in law school—the primary basis on which new law professors are hired.

It's good to get to know your professors. If a law professor likes you, she can help your career. This can include nominations for awards, research assistant positions and job recommendations.

Go visit your professors in their offices. Students mistakenly believe law professors are always busy inventing new legal theories, when it's just as likely they're trying to improve their free throw percentage with a Nerf® basketball or twisting paper clips into perfect isosceles triangles. Being a law professor can be an isolating life.

Most professors like it when students come talk to them.

Venturing into a professor's office can be intimidating, but relax. Here are some guaranteed ice-breakers for schmoozing your profs. The top five subjects of conversation most loved by law professors are:

1. **Their brains.**
2. **Their children.**
3. **Their children's brains.**
4. **Their brainy new law review article.**
5. **Their dean's lack of brains.**[12]

About the only surprise here may be the children. But make no mistake, law professors do have sex and do indeed have children. In fact, you need to know that LAW PROFESSORS HAVE INCREDIBLY ADORABLE CHILDREN. Law professors worship their children and believe they are entitled to equal treatment with adults. Infants and toddlers are common sights in classrooms, faculty meetings, committee meetings, just about everywhere. At some schools, children of faculty get to vote on promotion and tenure matters. On rare delightful moments, children can be found team-teaching classes with their parents.

To get in good with a professor, comment on how beautiful his or her child is, even if the kid is ugly as a moth. This simple gesture will endear you to the professor for life. If you offer to babysit, the professor is likely to nominate you for the law school's Professional Service Award.

---

[12] Of course, this does not include my dean—a brilliant man with many amazing abilities, including the ability to raise my salary.

However, be aware that law professors also believe strongly in children's rights, including the fundamental right of every tyke to rough up a babysitter.

Law professors are very idiosyncratic and it's difficult to pigeonhole them (although a mob of drunken students once tried with their Property professor). Four types of law professors turn up with regularity:

1. **The Performer.**
2. **The Legend.**
3. **The Radical Feminist.**
4. **The Strange Creature from Outer Space.**

A few words about each will be helpful.

The Performer

The most important goal of teaching for a Performer is laughs, followed by applause and the hope of someday replacing Letterman. Performers tend to be younger professors with a lot of energy. They're a lot of fun at student parties and, for a reasonable fee, weddings and bar mitzvahs. Most Performers are frustrated actors, but some are simply realists who've recognized that educating a generation of students who have been raised on flash and sizzle entertainment requires some nontraditional skills, such as juggling, magic tricks and a decent animal act.

Here's an excerpt from a Civil Procedure lecture taught by one of the nation's up-and-coming Performers:

Good afternoon and welcome to Civil Procedure. We have a terrific class lined up for you today, leading off with the famous case of *Pennoyer v. Neff.*

Get out! I'm kidding. We've got something a lot better than that. It's Tuesday and you know what that means. Stupid Law Student Tricks! Can Billy Joe Dufus explain the abstention doctrine with his thumb rammed into an electric socket? We'll learn the shocking answer live.

Our special guest today is our very own Dean Beancounter. [Loud boos] Stop, stop. He's not here to explain last week's forty percent tuition increase. I'm going to saw him in half. Illusion? You be the judge. Should we put him back together? We'll take your vote.

To get things rolling, it's my pleasure to introduce our first guest, the lovely second-year student with the rock-bottom LSAT® who stunned the critics in the surprise hit of last semester, Constitutional Law. She's currently getting rave reviews in the sequel, Con Law II. Please give a warm welcome to—hold it—we've got a call coming in on the Law Line ...

The best way to get answers to your legal questions from Performers is to include them as postscripts to fan mail.

The Legend

Every law school has at least one Legend, a distinguished professor who through decades, sometimes centuries, of lecturing and publishing has become known as the leading authority in his field. Actor John Houseman played a Legend to perfection in his immortal portrayal of the curmudgeony Professor Kingsfield in the *The Paper Chase*.[13] Legends have mastered what we all long to master: how to act like a bastard and still be loved. Through reputation, length of service and law school folklore, Legends receive adulation even though one of their few remaining pleasures in life is persecuting innocent students.

Look at this excerpt of a Socratic dialogue between a student and a distinguished Torts Legend concerning the famous case of *Rylands v. Fletcher*,[14] which teaches students the important legal rule that it's a bad idea to dig a reservoir over a bunch of coal mining shafts and fill it with ten trillion tons of water:

Professor:	**Mr. Frocklebean,**[15] **tell us the facts of** ***Rylands v. Fletcher.***
Mr. Finkelstein:	**Well, in this case, the plaintiff—**
Professor:	**Wrong!**
Mr. Finkelstein:	**But professor, you didn't let me finish. You don't even know what I was going to say.**

---

[13] Every law student should rent this classic flick.

[14] 1 Exchequer 265 (1866), 3 House of Lords 330 (1868).

[15] Student's real name is Finkelstein. Legends pride themselves on not pronouncing a single student's name correctly in 95 years.

Professor:	Mr. Frammerskein, I've been teaching this case for ninety-five years. No student has ever got it right. Are you telling us you're the most brilliant student to attend law school in ninety-five years? Is that what you're saying? I suppose you know all of the answers, Mr. Fragglerock, and the rest of us are complete idiots. Get the hell out of my classroom!

Amazingly, students view this conduct as quaint when it comes from an *elder person*.

The Radical Feminist

Before discussing Radical Feminist law professors, I want to clear up an important misconception about them. It is not true that Radical Feminists blame men for 100 percent of the things that go wrong in the universe. They only blame men for 92 percent of the things that go wrong in the universe, which is still grossly unfair since the actual figure is only 91 percent. Radical feminists believe our society operates under a "patriarchal paradigm" in which men hold most of the cards. They would have you believe that most presidents, generals, members of Congress, high-paid corporate executives and millionaire athletes are men. Some nerve.

Don't get me wrong. I love Radical Feminists. One of my best friends, Mary Pat Treuthart, is a Radical Feminist at a

law school in the Great Northwest. She teaches a course called *Women and the Law,* where a group of women students and one guy who grievously miscalculates that this is a great place to meet chicks get together to discuss gender issues. I once asked Mary Pat if there is any truth to the rumor that at the end of the semester they tie the guy up and set fire to him. She laughed at my naivete and said, "Of course not. Everyone knows cigarette burns don't ignite human flesh, stupid man." Of course, I'm kidding about all of this. I'm just peeved that women have figured out that most men are insensitive boors.

All law students—male and female—need to be sensitive about gender issues, especially in classes taught by a Radical Feminist. Refer to females only as "women." Don't use "lady" or "girl," and definitely not "babe." Refer to guys as "men," even if they usually act like "boys." In class discussions, it's safest to avoid gender pronouns altogether. Whenever possible, speak in completely gender-neutral terms. For example, if a professor asks you to explain a judge's ruling, say:

> **The judge—who could be a man or a woman or possibly even a child, or a cross-dresser or a transsexual or a woman-on-the-top-part-and-man-on-the-bottom-part or might not even be human— ruled that the defendant should win the case because he, ahem, excuse me, I mean, the defendant—who could be a man or a woman or possibly even a child or ...**

After years of pondering the issue, I decided that Radical Feminists are indeed correct about most issues regarding gender inequality, so I asked Mary Pat how I could go about becoming a Radical Feminist. She told me that, according to feminist doctrine, a man cannot be a feminist. At most, men can be only "pro-feminist." In my case, however, she recommended that I stick with the ideology of my birthright, stupid-manism.

The Strange Creature from Outer Space

As I already mentioned, law professors—like professors in all disciplines—are disproportionately odd. Eccentric characters? I know one obsessive-compulsive professor who can never say "It's very bizarre" just once. He always has to repeat it. If he doesn't say it twice, he breaks out in a sweat, goes into a panic attack and has the urge to jump in front of a train. It's very bizarre.

However, mixed in among the simply odd is a subgroup of aberrant human beings known as Strange Creatures from Outer Space, because that is the most plausible explanation for the way their brains work. The minds of Strange Creatures from Outer Space operate in ways that cannot be understood even by trained scientists, much less poor law students. All that is known for sure is that computerized magnetic resonance imaging of a Strange Creature's brain waves reveals images bearing an uncanny resemblance to: (1) an exploding galaxy; (2) holiday mall shoppers; and (3) all 535 members of Congress simultaneously spotting a free lunch buffet.

The classic mark of a Strange Creature is the inability to explain even elementary concepts so that they can be comprehended by anyone not suffering from schizophrenia. Part of the problem is that Strange Creatures are not linear thinkers. Their thoughts tend to emerge in bursts of fragmented energy, rather than as organized, deductive analysis. Instead of starting explanations at a logical place, such as the beginning, Strange Creatures prefer to start at the middle or end. You probably have friends like this— people who never learned how to "take it from the top" when telling a story—friends who open a story about a relationship breakup with, "So I shot him in the back and that was that."

While this is merely annoying when it comes from friends, it can be perilous when you are relying on a professor to explain a legal doctrine that could be on the exam. As an example, compare the relative difficulty of understanding the simple "mailbox rule" of contract law. A normal explanation starting at the beginning would say:

> **Let's talk about the mailbox rule. The rule is clear. This good rule of contract law states that, under normal circumstances, a written acceptance of a contract, if properly addressed and stamped and not later rejected, should be effective when it is actually deposited outside in the U.S. mail.**

Makes sense. But look how murky things get when a Strange Creature explains the rule by beginning at the end:

Let's talk about the mailbox rule. The rule is clear. It is actually deposited outside in the U.S. mail.

But it gets even worse because, in addition to beginning the explanation at the end, Strange Creatures then proceed to rearrange all the other parts. Thus, using the EXACT same words as in the first explanation, the Strange Creature's explanation of the mailbox rule might come out like this:

> It is actually ... clear ... outside. Good. The U.S. mail ... is ... not ... effective ... if properly addressed and stamped .... Under normal circumstances ... it ... should be ... rejected. Let's talk ... later.

Another difficulty with Strange Creatures is that, because they do not think logically, it is impossible for students to predict what they will consider to be important in a case. This means that no matter how diligently students read and brief their cases, they will be unprepared for class, as shown in this Socratic dialogue:

> **Strange Creature:** Mr. Klatu, tell us the single most important fact influencing the outcome of the court's decision to award damages to the plaintiff in this case.

Student:	Was it that the defendant pushed plaintiff off a cliff?
Strange Creature:	Irrelevant. Try again.
Student:	Um, maybe the fact that the defendant set up a trap of sharpened bamboo sticks where he landed?
Strange Creature:	I said important. Think!
Student:	That the defendant poured poison down plaintiff's throat after the fall?
Strange Creature:	No, no, no. What was the defendant wearing at the time of the act?
Student:	Wearing? I'm not sure.
Strange Creature:	You're not sure? You overlooked the most critical fact in the entire case! Look at line 24 of footnote 97 on page 873, where it says plain as day "the defendant was arrested wearing blood-stained yellow pants."
Student:	So?
Strange Creature:	So?!! Look at the date! The incident occurred in October. Can't you see it? Obviously, the court was so disgusted by the defendant's

gross fashion faux pas of
wearing yellow pants after
Labor Day that it simply
could not view the rest of
the case objectively.

Bless the hearts of law students. They are so indoctrinated
to believe in the brilliance of their professors that many of
them will dutifully write down "Don't wear yellow pants
after Labor Day" as the holding of the case.

So there you have four basic types of law professors.
Take them into consideration when registering for
courses. Pick professors who best match your own
personality. However, be aware that law professors are
complex beings who often spill over into more than one
category. If you're not careful, you could end up in a class
taught by a Legendary Strange Creature from Outer Space
who is a Performing Radical Feminist. If that happens, I
recommend you drop the course.

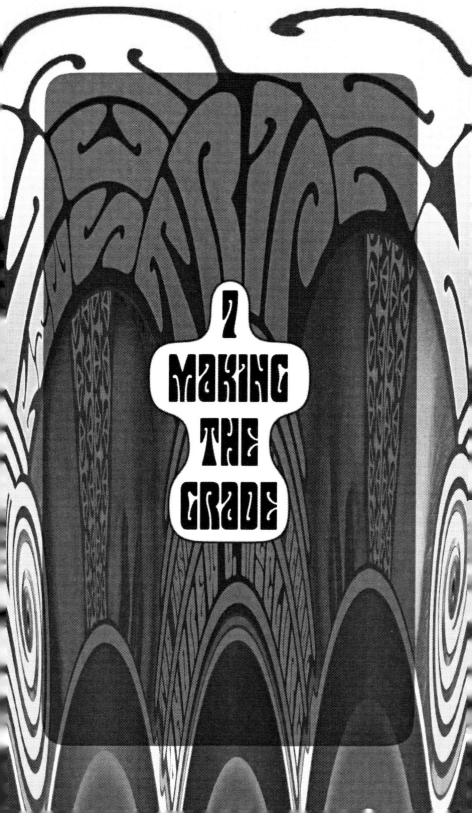

7
MAKING THE GRADE

etting good grades is the Holy Grail of law school. To a first-year law student, a "B+" in Contracts is worth more than 100,000 shares of Microsoft® stock. There are logical reasons for this phenomenon. Class rank and grade point average are the first things law firms look at in making hiring decisions, next to whether they think the applicant can make an immediate impact on the firm softball team.

But law schools also bear part of the blame for the obsession with grades. The entire reward structure at most law schools centers on getting good grades. Students with the best grades are invited to join the Law Review. They get awards for writing the top exam in a class. They get scholarships. They get positions working as research assistants to professors.

Students also contribute to the problem because they are disproportionately high-achieving, competitive people, driven to succeed. Indeed, the level of competitiveness that exists among law students is the highest in the world according to two new competing studies about competitiveness. Here are the top five competitive activities according to the surveys, in reverse order:

Top Five Competitive Activities

5. The Olympics.
4. Who can commit the most traffic infractions while driving a Sport Utility Vehicle and talking on a cell phone.
3. Which neighborhood dog can howl the loudest at night.
2. Nuclear war.
1. Law school.

Although law students develop many unhealthy obsessions and anxieties, getting good grades is easily number one on both lists. Since law school makes everyone anal-retentive, we have the benefit of having actual lists to empirically support this proposition:

Things to Obsess About

1. Getting an "A."
2. Developing a stress-related substance abuse problem.
3. Paying back $100,000 in student loans if I can't get a job.
4. Having a panic attack if I get called on.
5. The Rule Against Perpetuities.

Things to be Anxious About

1. Getting an "F."
2. Running out of beer and heroin.
3. Paying back $100,000 in student loans even if I do get a job.

4. ????? Can't remember … can't think!!!
5. The Rule Against Perpetuities.

The law school grading system aggravates the situation. In most law school classes, the grade for the entire course is based on one lengthy essay exam at the end of the semester, make it or break it. Students receive no other feedback during the course. Every once in a while a brave student will ask the reason behind this great tradition. One official explanation is that giving periodic tests or quizzes during the semester would distract students from studying for their other courses, which really is a legitimate concern. However, another explanation, given credence by many law professors, is historically rooted. Grading lengthy essay exams is time-consuming and tedious. Few sights are more daunting than a stack of 500 exam blue books. Rumor has it that the very first law professor figured this out and decided to give only one exam. Being brilliant, the other professors quickly recognized he had come up with a heckuva great tradition.

Because grades are so critical, some advice about how to perform well on exams is essential.

Study Tips

Take Good Notes. Perhaps the single best study tip I can give incoming law students is to take good notes in class. Law professors love to see their words in print, and having students regurgitate them on an exam is far easier than getting them published. The most reliable sign of a

brilliant student is one who appreciates the professor's spoken wisdom.

Law students will tell you we expect way too much. They say (and sing in their new music video): "I can't write down everything my professors say. They talk a blue streak and I write really slow. Plus, the things they talk about are so complicated that I don't even know what I'm writing down most of the time."

They have a valid point. For example, in Property you'll learn about the Rule Against Perpetuities, already mentioned above as a major source of both obsession and anxiety. The Rule Against Perpetuities is the most bizarre and hilarious rule in all of law. Ha, ha. I'm laughing just thinking about it. For one thing, no other legal rule has doctrines that sound like old blues tunes. The "Bad as to One, Bad as to All" and "Unborn Widow" rules could have been classic hits for Muddy Waters.

But the main reason the Rule Against Perpetuities is so hilarious is that no one understands it. Yet every lawyer still vividly remembers not-learning the rule. Studies show that all the average lawyer knows about the Rule Against Perpetuities is that, for reasons never fully developed, "21 years" is important to property law.

The rule is so impossibly complex that the distinguished California Supreme Court once suggested a lawyer cannot be guilty of malpractice for misapplying it.[16] However, my

---

[16] In *Lucas v. Hamm*, 364 P.2d 685 (Cal. 1975), the court rejected a malpractice claim against an attorney arising from an alleged misapplication of the Rule Against Perpetuities, stating:

The complaint, as we have seen, alleges that defendant drafted the will in such a manner that the trust was invalid because it violated the rules relating to perpetuities and restraints on alienation. These

colleague who teaches property law assures me that people can and do get sued for violating the Rule Against Perpetuities; it's just that no one can ever figure out why. The good news is that because so few people understand the rule, it is seldom tested either in law school or on the bar exam.

The Rule Against Perpetuities has to do with how a deceased person can control the future ownership rights of her property by complicated provisions in a will or trust. Here's how a law professor would define the rule in a class lecture:

RULE AGAINST PERPETUITIES:

No contingent future interest in a transferee is good unless it must vest or fail to vest within 21 years of the death of some life in being at the time of the creation of the interest.

RATIONALE IS STRAIGHTFORWARD—The rule is designed to limit efforts by grantors to restrict the free alienation of property by burdening it with contingent future interests.

THE SIMPLE WAY to understand the rule is to remember that it all has to do with the vesting or failure to vest of a contingent future interest within the lifetime of a measuring life or 21 years after that person's death.

---

closely akin subjects have long perplexed the courts and the bar. Professor Gray, a leading authority in the field, stated: 'There is something in the subject which seems to facilitate error. Perhaps it is because the mode of reasoning is unlike that with which lawyers are most familiar. . . . A long list might be formed of the demonstrable blunders with regard to its

Here's what a law student's class notes from the exact same lecture would look like:

RULE AGAINST PERPETOOTIES:
    No astringent foosball interest ??
... must vest OR FAIL TO VEST...
21 years ... death ... life in bean???
Creation? interest ?????
    PROF. SAYS RATIONALE
STRAIGHTFORWARD —
    Rule designed to limit
grantees ORS ... something, something,
something...
    SLOW THE * * * * DOWN!!
alien nation of Property???
    SIMPLE WAY to understand
rule is to remember that it all
has to do with ...
    BUY PROPERTY FLASHCARDS!!!
... 21 years, 21 years, 21 years...
    Prof. says don't worry about.
NOT ON TEST!!! NOT MALPRACTICE.

questions made by eminent men, ... and there are few lawyers of any practice in drawing wills and settlements who have not at some time either fallen into the net which the Rule spreads for the unwary, or at least shuddered to think how narrowly they have escaped it.' Of the California law on perpetuities and restraints it has been said that few, if any, areas of the law have been fraught

Most students' notes resemble these, so don't be alarmed if yours do. The amazing thing is that some students really do manage to write down every word spoken by a professor. Look at these outstanding Contracts notes compiled by a stellar student:

> ## Coleen's Contracts Notes
> ## — Fall Semester —
> ### REWARD IF FOUND!
>
> Day One: Good morning. Welcome to Contracts. I'm Professor Dorkman. Anybody got any Ibuprofen®? My head is killing me. You wouldn't believe the night I had last night. It's drafty in here. Someone shut that window over there. Is that clock right?

…[20 more pages]

---

with more confusion or concealed more traps for the unwary draftsman. . . . In view of the state of the law relating to perpetutities . . . , it would not be proper to hold that defendant failed to use such skill, prudence, and diligence as lawyers of ordinary skill and capacity commonly exercise. Id. at 690.

Day Two: My daughter did the most darling thing this morning. Projectile vomiting in an amazing geometric pattern. She is extremely advanced at regurgitation for her age. I'm getting ready to show you a Power Point presentation of it. Have I told you how cute my daughter is?

...[30 more pages]

Day Three: Okay, let's talk about contract law. Contract law involves the formation and breaches of agreements. Which reminds me of a joke. A lawyer walks into a bar with a duck on a leash. The bartender says to

...[40 more pages]

Needless to say, the student earned the top grade in the course for her ability to recognize and record such words of sagacity.

Join A Study Group. A popular law school study method is the study group. The primary benefit of a study group is group sharing. A common study group technique is the division of labor method, whereby each member of the group is assigned to prepare an outline for a particular course. At the end of the semester, the study group members exchange their outlines and all bases are covered.

You need to be extremely selective in choosing members for a study group, especially if you intend to use a division of labor approach. Some groups make the mistake of selecting members based on criteria such as whether the person is hot-looking or is always willing to bring the beer. While these factors aren't insignificant, they rarely prove to be a benefit come exam time.

One weak link can destroy the effectiveness of the entire group, which allegedly happened in my own study group. A week before exams, all the members of our group exchanged the outlines we had worked on all semester. Each outline was more than 200 pages, except for the one intended to cover the complex course of Civil Procedure. The entire outline for this course read:

Civil Procedure Outline

I think the professor should be commended for doing a darn good job explaining this course. I don't really have anything to add.

The study group was extremely upset, but I really didn't have anything to add.

Buy Commercial Study Aids. There is probably only one study tip on which law students unanimously agree: BUY COMMERCIAL STUDY AIDS. These are course-specific books written especially for law students that define and explain the law in clear and succinct terms. A quality study aid can lucidly condense the entire first year of Property to fewer pages than the class notes you'll take on the Rule in Shelley's Case.

As a law professor with a lifetime membership in the Academy of Law Professors Devoted to Making the Law Confusing as Hell, I could get in big trouble for recommending study aids to you. Many law professors detest commercial study aids and will pitch a fit if they lay eyes on one. Why? Because the goal of legal education—especially at the best law schools—is not to teach the law, but to teach students to *think about* the law. Teaching law and teaching how to think about law are two very different things.

We can use the "one free bite" rule of tort law to demonstrate the difference. This rule says a dog owner is responsible for bite injuries inflicted by his pet, but only if the owner knew or had reason to know the dog was dangerous. Often, such knowledge can be inferred only

if the dog has previously bitten someone; hence, the name "one free bite" rule. Let's compare and contrast the commercial study aid method for teaching law with the law school method.

Commercial Study Aid Method
for Teaching One Free Bite Rule

A dog owner is liable for damages when his dog bites someone if the owner knew or had reason to know of the animal's dangerous propensities.

Law School Method
for Teaching One Free Bite Rule

Is there really such thing as a free bite? After all, what is "free"? Are you free? Am I free? To understand this rule, we must deconstruct the essence of freedom. Certainly, the bite is not always free from the doggie's perspective. What if a broken tooth results? Should the mutt then have a cause of action against the bitee? And what of the global perspective of canine freedom? Is your golden retriever free? Is he imbued with the autonomy essential to any definition of freedom? Does he have freedom of movement, the freedom to eat when he chooses, the freedom to defecate on the carpet? What good is a free bite without the freedom even to unlock the gate and go for a run around the neighborhood? Perhaps the rule was

intended to appease the canine masses by throwing them a bone, if you will, thus perpetuating their subjugation. Yes? No? These are obviously important questions. We'll devote the rest of the semester to them.

One final tip: When purchasing study aids, always go with reliable brand names like *Gilbert's Torts* and *Emmanuel's Contracts*. Avoid budget study aids like *Zoe's Class Notes* and *Jim Bob's Cheat Sheet*.

PRODUCT WARNING: NEVER RELY SOLELY ON STUDY AIDS. INTENDED FOR SUPPLEMENTAL USE ONLY. ALWAYS READ AND BRIEF YOUR CASES LIKE GOOD DO-BEES. AUTHOR NOT RESPONSIBLE FOR FAILING GRADES.

Test Taking

A startling discovery in the field of education theory is sending shock waves through student bodies around the nation. Researchers have finally confirmed what many educators have long suspected: that a statistically significant correlation exists between possessing knowledge and doing well on a test. Accordingly, although some students remain skeptical, studying is once again in vogue as a technique for successful educational performance. Henceforth, grade appeals based on reasons such as "was on vacation" or "forgot to buy books" are no longer expected to carry persuasive weight. Here are some other valuable suggestions for making the grade come test time:

1. Use Stress Reduction Techniques. Reducing your stress level is key to performing well on tests. Scientists have done studies analyzing the brain waves of both stressed and non-stressed (heavily medicated) law students taking exams. Look at the results:

Brain Wave Analysis of Non-stressed (Heavily Medicated) Student:

"Yawn. I count at least thirty complex issues in this essay question. The instructions say to 'fully analyze' each issue, but we only have an hour. Ha, ha. That's impossible. But I don't know the answers anyway, so that should save a lot of time. This isn't so bad."

Brain Wave Analysis of Stressed Student:

#&&_$*^(*$_)*_$&*)(^#*(*)^8)*%&&^@&*(&)*($*()
(@&()$&*)($*@()$*)(&%)*(&)(#%@%&^$@
%^$#^%$#%^@$%#$^$%^$#^(*%%(*&#(
)*(+) ($+*)^*&^)+*^$*&#%&^%#&^%#.

What's the best way to relax? Deep-breathing and stretching exercises have been shown to be effective, especially when performed on an island beach while drinking a pina colada. Another proven stress reduction technique is acupuncture. Sticking needles into carefully selected body parts—especially those belonging to professors—makes most law students feel much better.

2. Bring Proper Supplies to Exam. Part of being "well prepared" for an exam is bringing the necessary supplies with you, not just the basics like blue books and pens, but other useful items such as ear plugs, Wite-Out® and a 12-pack of Surge.®

Many students also bring in a good luck charm of some type, a situation that, frankly, is getting out of hand. The problem is getting so bad I anticipate having to implement "carry-in" restrictions similar to the "carry-on" rules that have proven so effective in the airline industry. Look at the items my students in the front row brought for good luck to the most recent Torts exam:

Student 1: Rabbit's foot, four-leaf clover, bucket of salt, ham radio.

Student 2: Poisonous cobra in wicker basket, Tiki idol, lottery ticket, autographed picture of Amazing Kreskin.

Student 3: Life-size marble Buddha.

Student 4: Distinguished Torts professor from another university.

Student 5: The answer.

3. Write In Legalese. It's important to write your exams in a formal fashion, using the technical language of the law. Do not use an overly breezy or conversational tone. An essay exam answer is a legal document and should read like one. Be precise in your legal analysis. Compare two contrasting approaches to answering a Torts question involving the issue of "transferred intent," an issue that, like a lot of legal issues, shows up frequently on law school

exams and the bar exam, but which almost never happens in real life.

Good Answer

This question raises the issue of *transferred intent* in a self-defense context. A shot at B with a 9mm pistol and missed, wounding C in the arm. C retaliated by picking up a rock and throwing it at A, inflicting a head injury.

The rule of transferred intent holds that if an actor intends to a commit a tort against one person (in this case, battery) but ends up committing the same tort against another person, her intent will transfer from the first person to the second person. Under this doctrine, A's intent to commit a battery against B carries over to the battery against C. Therefore, A is liable to C.

However, after being shot, C retaliated by throwing the rock and hitting A. C might claim self-defense. However, this argument will fail. Self-defense is a privilege to use reasonable force to prevent a threatened battery and not a privilege of retaliation. Since the battery upon C was already complete, C was not privileged to use force in self-defense. Therefore, C is liable to A for the injury from the rock.

Bad Answer

A capped C with his 9, which turned out to be a major ****-up because he was aiming at another dude. C got aggro and chucked a rock at A, knocking him upside the head. Cha-ching. The law doesn't let you go around shooting people—especially the wrong people—so the judge is going to stick it to A. On the other hand, maybe C deserved to get popped. The question doesn't say. Whatever, although I think it's a stupid rule, I'm pretty sure you said in class that you can't nail a guy with a rock just because he wings you with a pistol. A and C will both have to cough up big bucks.

4. Go By What Your Professor Says. Another important exam tip to remember is that THE LAW IS WHATEVER YOUR PROFESSOR SAYS IT IS. This is true even if the professor is dead wrong. It doesn't matter if every other source in the universe disagrees because these other sources aren't grading your exam.

If your Criminal Law professor tells you murder is legal in 14 states, go with it. If your Torts professor is pro-plaintiff, always conclude that the plaintiff should win, no matter how stupidly he has contributed to his own injuries. If the plaintiff shoots himself in the foot, suggest a lawsuit against the shoe manufacturer for negligently failing to make its cross-trainers out of Kevlar®. If your Constitutional Law professor is strongly pro-choice, work reproductive rights into your exam answer even if it's not

the issue. For example, if the issue is A's standing to sue, suggest the whole controversy could have been avoided if A's mom had exercised her constitutional right to choose.

Law Review

The ultimate achievement in law school is "making the law review." Law reviews are journals that publish scholarly legal articles written by professors, lawyers and students. Every law school has a law review. Wealthy schools also have lots of esoteric specialty journals like the *Journal of Useless Esoterica* and the *Wasted Pulp Law Review*. This is good because the more journals a school publishes, the better your odds of becoming a member of one of them.

The most outstanding students are invited to become law review "apprentices." If they do enough menial labor, they're extended the privilege of becoming "members." The most ambitious members are selected to be "Editors of the Law Review," a title equivalent to Starship Captain among competitive law students.

Becoming a law review member requires a tremendous amount of work. Law review apprentices are expected to produce at least one scholarly paper of publishable quality, as well as assist the editors in whatever capacity they see as necessary to the smooth functioning of the law review: fixing their breakfast, washing their pantyhose, caddying, whatever it takes.

The most arduous and time-consuming task assigned to law review apprentices is called "cite-checking." This

involves checking footnotes for accuracy. Law professors worship footnotes. If you took the footnotes out of a 300-page law review article, it would only be one paragraph. Law review articles look something like this:

This[1] is[2] the[3] world's[4] great[5]est[6] law[7] re[8]view[9] art[10]i[11]cle[12] be[13]cause[14] I[15] have[16] foot[17]not[18]ed[19] ev[20]er[21]y[22] sin[23]gle[24] syll[25]a[26]ble.[27] [17]

All footnotes must conform to the *Bluebook*, a style manual so extraordinarily complex and bizarre that it warrants its own chapter, coming up next.

As reward for their years of devoted service to the law review, members get a nice piece of paper at graduation that says, "Joe was on the Law Review." If your name's not Joe, tough luck. Kidding. They put your real name on it, but law review is a lot of work with few tangible rewards.

You may be thinking, "Gee, law review doesn't sound that great to me. I wonder why students are so anxious to get on it?" One reason is that being a member of the law review is a gravy ticket to a good job. Getting on law review makes a person very marketable, virtually guaranteeing employment with a prestigious law firm, no matter what else the applicant has done. Look at the résumé of a fellow recently hired as an associate at a big-city firm at a whopping beginning salary in excess of $100,000:

---

[17] Surely you didn't expect me to pass up the opportunity to footnote to a footnote.

MARKY "MARK THE SHARK" GAMBINI

EMPLOYMENT HISTORY:

1997-Present
License Plate Craftsperson,
State Correctional Facility

1995-96
Loan Collection Specialist,
Corleone & Associates

1989-94
Negotiated merger agreements for
Naughty Nancy and Delilah Delight

1985-88
Wagering Specialist
Fast Eddie, Inc.

PROFESSIONAL HONORS:
Highest reward for capture ever offered by county
sheriff; Undefeated in knife fights (44-0).

HOBBIES:
Setting fires, harming small animals.

LAW SCHOOL HONORS:
LAW REVIEW!

If you don't make the law review, don't sweat it too
much. Most of the richest lawyers didn't either.

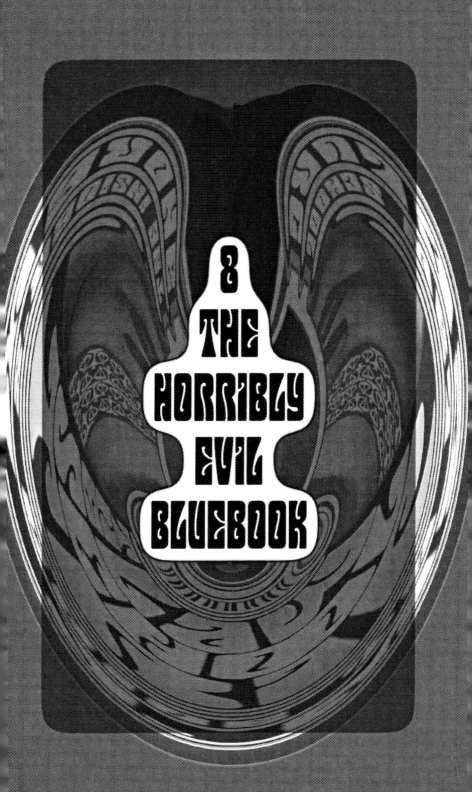

8
THE
HORRIBLY
EVIL
BLUEBOOK

hh, the *Bluebook*. How can one best describe the *Bluebook*, especially when brain-exploding confusion is so difficult to capture in print? The *Bluebook* is a 391-page manual that sets forth the standards of style and citation to be used throughout legal writing. It covers rules for punctuation, abbreviation and, most importantly, the rules for correctly citing to statutes, cases, constitutions and other legal authorities. All law students are expected to master the *Bluebook* in their first-year legal research course.[18]

The *Bluebook* is the most hypertechnical text ever written. It makes the maintenance manual for the Hubble Space Telescope read like a Golden Book®. The nit-picking complexity of the *Bluebook* over minutiae such as spacing, typeface and punctuation seems

---

[18] In 2000, the Association of Legal Writing Directors published a new style manual to compete with the *Bluebook*. *See* ASS'N OF LEGAL WRITING DIRECTORS & DARBY DICKERSON, ALWD CITATION MANUAL, A PROFESSIONAL SYSTEM OF CITATION (2000). The *ALWD Citation Manual* is intended to greatly simplify legal citations. It differs radically from the *Bluebook*, primarily in the fact that it is green and white and 80 pages longer. Seriously, my legal writing colleague gave me her rough estimate that the *ALWD Citation Manual* is 58.434 percent easier to use than the *Bluebook*. A growing number of schools are forsaking the *Bluebook* in favor of the new *ALWD Citation Manual*, making this perhaps the most important factor to consider in selecting a law school. However, since we're safe within a footnote, I'll make another confession. Despite all the jokes, I love the *Bluebook*.

intentionally designed to trip up even the most anal-retentive student. But why believe me? See for yourself in this real *Bluebook* rule explaining, believe it or not, how to cite to a footnote in a footnote:

> **Rule 3.3(b) Footnotes.** To cite to a footnote, give the page on which the footnote appears, "n.," and the footnote number, with no space between "n." and the number ... To cite all of a footnote that spans more than one page, cite only the page on which the footnote begins, "n.," and the footnote number.... When referring only to specific pages of a footnote that spans more than one page, cite only the specific pages, rather than the page on which the footnote begins.[19]

What's the purpose of the *Bluebook*? One critic explained it this way:

> **The *Blue Book* [sic] ... champions *technical due process*. According to this doctrine, it does not matter who wrote the article; it does not matter how he wrote it. It does not matter what the article says, it does not matter that it says nothing**

---

[19] THE BLUEBOOK: A UNIFORM SYSTEM OF CITATION 35 (17th ed. 2000) (Rule 3.3(b)).

LOOK AT THE CITATION TO THE BLUEBOOK. DID YOU NOTICE THE STRANGE TYPEFACE OF BIG AND SMALL CAPITAL LETTERS? According to the *Bluebook*, this is CRITICALLY IMPORTANT. Rule 15.1.2. I had to beg the publishers not to change the typeface. They acquiesced only when I produced sworn affidavits from *Bluebook* experts that my life could be in jeopardy for violating such an important footnoting convention.

at all. The doctrine of technical due process maintains that *if the footnotes are wrong, the article is worthless.*[20]

Who's behind the *Bluebook*? Ask a law student and she'll say, "A group of inherently evil law review editors destined to spend eternity in a Sisyphean *supra-infra* citation loop." To find out whether this is true, we went undercover. At great personal risk, one of my staff successfully infiltrated and recorded the proceedings of the Ivy League Committee on Uniform Citation on a historic occasion, a meeting that forever changed the fate of millions of innocent lawyers and law students. That's right. I'm talking about the night the *Bluebook* editors met to create Rule 15.2, which mandates in profound language:

If the title of a work ends with a numeral, the page number must be set off by a comma....

Here, for the first time ever, is the complete story of Rule 15.2 and its infamous comma as told by the actual meeting transcript. The meeting opened with Editor-In-Chief Irving Frunk explaining the merits of his proposal to the other editors:

Irving: We need that #*%##&* comma!
Rule 15.2 means nothing without
The Comma. I'll gladly die for it.

---

[20] Alan Strasser, *Technical Due Process:?*, 12 HARVARD CIVIL RIGHTS-CIVIL LIBERTIES LAW REVIEW 507 (1977).

Frieda: *Accord.*[21]

Dan: *Accord.*

Wendy: Put down the gun, Irving. The *Bluebook* was meant to bring peace.

Irving: Not until I have proof of everyone's commitment to The Comma. I've decided to quit law school and become addicted to amphetamines so I can contemplate The Comma twenty-four hours a day.

Dan: I'm going to have Rule 15.2 tattooed on my thigh, right below the rules for Separately Bound Legislative Histories.

Frieda: I'll cut out my husband's entrails and form them into the shape of one huge comma.

Irving: What about you Wendy?

Wendy: My parents died in a plane crash yesterday. I have to go to the funeral.

Irving: Doesn't The Comma mean anything to you?

Wendy: Alright, I'll send flowers.

Irving: Fantastic. We're all behind The Comma. But before we can

---

[21] *Bluebook* editors like to speak in the language of the great work itself. *Accord* is a "signal" used as a preface to legal authority that directly supports a proposition. *See* Rule 1.2.

officially adopt it, we're obligated under our Non-Discrimination Policy to give equal consideration to the period, exclamation point and question mark.

Wendy: What about umlauts? They've never gotten a fair shake. We don't have a single umlaut in the entire *Bluebook*. It might be a nice change.

Frieda: That's *sick*. Shoot her, Irving. She doesn't love The Comma like the rest of us. We don't need change. We need The Comma. The Comma is the only possible answer. And to give it dignity, we must enshrine it in parentheses.

Dan: I have an even better idea. Let's put *a hundred* commas in a row! Look at this.

Dan distributes the following draft of his proposal:

,,,,,,,,,,,,,,,,,,,,,,,,,,,,,,,
,,,,,,,,,,,,,,,,,,,,,,,,,,,,,,,
,,,,,,,,,,,,,,,,,,,,,,,,,,,,,,,

Dan: Isn't it glorious? Think of the symbolism. Commas giving birth to commas, bursting onto the next page, into the next generation and beyond. Let's make it a thousand.

Ten thousand! Commas for infinity. Commas for ...

Irving: Easy, Dan. Slow down. First we need to get everyone obsessing about The Comma, then we'll be free to do as we please. It's been a long night. We need food and rest. We'll reconvene at sunrise to draft a preamble to The Comma. Let's close with our traditional blessing. Place your hands on the *Bluebook* ...
Thank you for 391 pages of stability and truth. And thank you for The Comma.[22]

DISCLAIMER: This is a work of fiction. All characters and punctuation described herein are either invented or used fictitiously, except of course for The Comma, which is all too real.

---

[22] *And thank you for footnotes. Amen.*

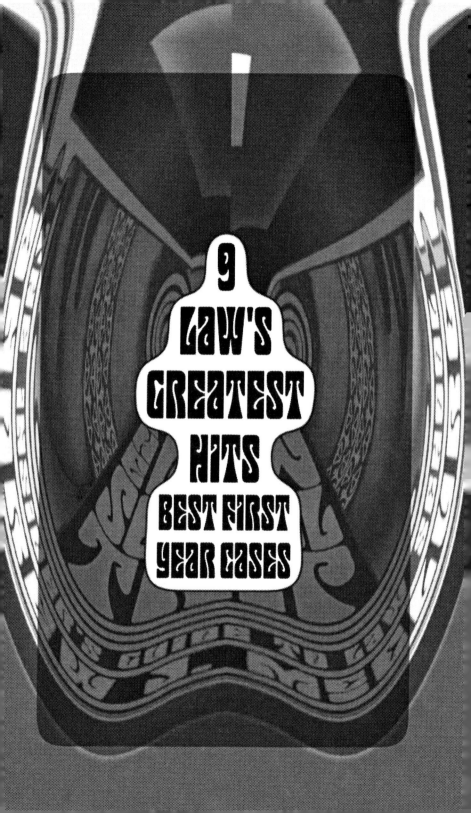

I n law school you will acquire far more knowledge than in any other period of your life, more than you ever dreamed possible. That much is guaranteed. Upon graduation, your brain will be bursting with so many rules, doctrines and theories you'll want to crack it open with a pick ax to relieve the pressure.

PRODUCT WARNING: DO NOT CRACK HEAD OPEN WITH PICK AX. AUTHOR NOT RESPONSIBLE FOR SELF-INFLICTED HEAD INJURIES. NOT COVERED BY MOST PICK AX WARRANTIES.

The sad part is you won't remember much of this knowledge. The old maxim is true: "You'll never know more law than the day you take the bar exam." It all goes rapidly downhill from there. The second the bar exam is over, your memory starts flushing out all those rules, doctrines and theories faster than you can say *res ipsa loquitur*,[23] if you can still remember it, which you probably won't be able to.

Go ahead. Test my theory. Approach any lawyer on the street and ask her to state the Rule in Shelley's Case or

---

[23] For readers who haven't made it through the first semester, *res ipsa loquitur* is a famous doctrine of tort law that translates to "the thing speaks for itself," in which case we don't need to be wasting precious footnotes discussing it.

explain *Marbury v. Madison*. You'll just get a blank stare (and perhaps pepper-sprayed) even though these topics consume major portions of a law student's life.

You might find it surprising that lawyers retain so little of the knowledge they acquire in law school, but there's actually a sound medical explanation for the phenomenon. It's a well-known scientific fact that the human brain retains only a small percentage of what it learns, in the range of 10 to 20 percent.

So think about it. You're a human brain. You're only able to retain, we'll be generous, 20 percent of everything you process. This means you're able to remember only one in five thoughts, which in turn means lots of tough choices about what to remember and what to forget. With a ratio of only one in five, a lot of perfectly good thoughts are going to be forgotten, perhaps unfairly.

To better understand this medical concept and how it works against remembering legal knowledge, we performed computer-enhanced magnetic resonance imaging of a law student's brain in action. At the time of the experiment, five thoughts were colliding in the student's memory zone, competing to be remembered:

1. The 29 exceptions to the hearsay rule.
2. Rule 12(b)(6) of the Federal Rules of Civil Procedure.
3. The Statute of Frauds.
4. Location of lost class notes to Criminal Law.
5. Location of legal fraternity keg party.

It wasn't much of a contest. Thoughts 4 and 5 tussled briefly before No. 5 tossed No. 4 out the earhole (No. 5 fell victim to the same process in a later memory contest, won with embarrassing ease by the phone number of a cute second-year student.)

But with that all said, there are a handful of cases that lawyers never forget. These are the true classics, cases that live on in the memories of all lawyers for eternity. If the law were music, these nuggets would make up *Law's Greatest Hits* and form the backbone of *Law: The Box Set (Digitally remastered on 24,000,000,000 compact discs)*. All the true greatest hits are studied in the first year. Every first-year course has at least one of these classics. Get a jump on the competition by learning about them in advance.

Torts: *Palsgraf v. Long Island Railroad,*
248 N.Y. 339, 162 N.E. 99 (N.Y. Court of Appeals 1928)

Let's begin with *Palsgraf,* a case about an exploding package of fireworks that knocked a heavy scale on top of poor Mrs. Helen Palsgraf at the Long Island train station in 1924. *Palsgraf* is the undisputed heavyweight champion in the field of tort law and perhaps the most memorable case from all of law school. To test this theory, go the intensive care ward of a hospital. Find a 98-year-old lawyer in a coma gasping for his last breath. Shout *"Palsgraf!"* The immediate response will be: "Two men were running for a train. One carried a box wrapped in newspaper … cough, cough … *Ack.*"

To appreciate *Palsgraf*'s stature, consider that the legendary *Prosser* Torts casebook includes four pictures of the case. Pop-ups! Kidding about the pop-ups, but the book really does have four pictures of *Palsgraf* and pictures are rare in law books. If you like books with pictures, especially pictures of diseased organs, go to medical school. The four *Palsgraf* pictures in Dean Prosser's famous casebook show: a scale like the one that fell on Mrs. P, the railway platform where the accident occurred and Judges Benjamin Cardozo and William Andrews, the two legal giants who wrote opposing opinions in the case. A picture of Dean Prosser's cute little kitty cat was edited out by the publisher.

Palsgraf is famous alright, but it's also a crock. You heard it right. The most famous case in Torts history is a sham. Before explaining, I need to relate the epiphany leading to this conclusion.

Here is one of the only true stories in this book (truth, of course, being a relative concept). Like all law students, I blindly believed *Palsgraf* was of supreme importance to tort law because my Torts professor said it was and we discussed it in class interminably. When I became a law professor, I had no reason to question this assumption. Like all law professors, I taught *Palsgraf* as if it were religious scripture unlocking the secrets of the universe instead of what it really is—a preposterous case mucking up the field of negligence law. That was until I met Rick the bartender.

One evening while teaching as a visiting professor in San Francisco, I went to the Haight-Ashbury district to celebrate the 30th anniversary of the Summer of Love. After breaking up a fight between two skinheads, I wandered into a dark

bar on Haight Street where I met Rick the bartender.

PRODUCT WARNING: RICK IS NOT HIS REAL NAME. AUTHOR NOT RESPONSIBLE FOR LIBEL TO PERSONS WITH NAMES, ALIASES, *NOMS DE PLUME*, MONICKERS, "HELLO, MY NAME IS _____" LABELS, DOG TAGS, TATTOOS OR E-MAIL ADDRESSES, INCLUDING OR IN ANY WAY RESEMBLING, RICK, RICHARD, RICH, DICK, RICKY, RICKMEISTER OR ANY OTHER NAME LISTED IN THE BIG BOOK OF 100,000 BABY NAMES.

Rick, it turns out, was a lawyer. He hated practicing law so much that he quit after six years to tend bar at a complete dive. He did not hold the practice of law in high regard. When I made the mistake of mentioning I was a law professor who teaches Torts, I discovered he had even lower regard for legal education. Rick harbored a particularly ugly vendetta against *Palsgraf*.

"And what's up with *Palsgraf*?" Rick snarled while mixing a martini for a woman with purple hair and enough body piercings to make a set of quality Craftsman® lawn tools. "There's a real piece of ****! Give me one good reason why law professors spend two weeks going on and on about a case that can be summed up in one ******* sentence. 'You're not liable for accident injuries if the harm wasn't foreseeable.' That's all the case says. Why don't professors just come out and say that? What kind of horse **** is that?"

I weakly tried to defend *Palsgraf*, but the truth of Rick's

words touched a nerve. Sensing the advantage, Rick yelled even louder. The purple-haired woman with the hedge trimmers in her eyebrow shouted "**** *Palsgraf*!" and smashed her martini glass on the floor. Pretty soon the entire bar was dissing Mrs. P and exhorting Rick to drop a scale on me.

The problem was I knew Rick was right. *Palsgraf* troubled me even as a law student. I was just too afraid to question it. The next day, I told my Torts students we were going to skip the most famous case in Torts history. They cheered me for my courage, my progressiveness and for cutting 15 pages from their reading assignment.

How was I supposed to know the main question on the bar exam that year would be about some exploding fireworks that knocked a shopping cart onto a woman?[24] But it wasn't a 7 percent bar passage rate that persuaded me to reinstate *Palsgraf* in all its glory. The truth is, I missed Mrs. Palsgraf. Who wouldn't after the weekend we spent together at the Cape? No, what I really missed was THE MOST FAMOUS CASE IN TORTS HISTORY. Life didn't seem complete without it, particularly the two-week hole in my syllabus.

Few law professors are as enlightened as Rick the bartender, so you might as well start learning about that fateful day in August 1924 at the Long Island train station. No one could improve on the terse factual description given by the great Judge Benjamin Cardozo:

---

[24] Sorry to interrupt, but a friend of mine read this part and wrote "OOH!" in the margin, so I feel compelled to explain that this part of the story is NOT TRUE.

Plaintiff was standing on a platform of defendant's railroad after buying a ticket to go to Rockaway Beach. A train stopped at the station, bound for another place. Two men ran forward to catch it. One of the men reached the platform of the car without mishap, though the train was already moving. The other man, carrying a package, jumped aboard the car, but seemed unsteady as if about to fall. A guard on the car, who had held the door open, reached forward to help him in, and another guard on the platform pushed him from behind. In this act, the package was dislodged, and fell upon the rails. It was a package of small size, about fifteen inches long, and covered by a newspaper. In fact it contained fireworks, but there was nothing in its appearance to give notice of its contents. The fireworks when they fell exploded. The shock of the explosion threw down some scales at the other end of the platform many feet away. The scales struck the plaintiff, causing injuries for which she sues.[25]

Helen Palsgraf sued the railroad, claiming the guards were negligent in knocking loose the package, which caused it to explode and tip the scale onto her. As mentioned, two famous judges—Benjamin Cardozo and William Andrews—wrote opinions in the case, Cardozo for the majority and Andrews in dissent. For 70 years, 1Ls everywhere have been forced to try to unravel these

[25] 248 N.Y. at 340-41, 162 N.E. at 99.

legendary, but exceedingly complex opinions. Cardozo's opinion ruled for the railroad, concluding the guards owed no legal duty to protect Mrs. Palsgraf from harm because they could not reasonably foresee the package presented a danger to her. Sound simple? Ha, ha. Wait until you read Cardozo's opinion.

Andrews wrote a dissent disagreeing with Cardozo. Andrews said everyone owes a legal duty to everyone else in the world to protect them from harm, but that a defendant isn't liable if his conduct isn't the proximate cause of the plaintiff's injury. One of Andrews' great contributions to the law is the following convoluted hypothetical he offered in his *Palsgraf* dissent:

> **A chauffeur negligently collides with another car which is filled with dynamite, although he could not know it. An explosion follows. A, walking on the sidewalk nearby, is killed. B, sitting in a window of a building opposite, is cut by flying glass. C, likewise sitting in a window a block away, is similarly injured. And a further illustration: A nursemaid, ten blocks away, startled by the noise, involuntarily drops a baby from her arms to the walk.[26]**

This hypothetical is guaranteed to stimulate hours and hours and hours and hour and hours and hours of classroom discussion, because some Torts teachers won't have it any other way.

---

[26] 248 N.Y. at 353, 162 N.E. at 104 (Andrews, J., dissenting).

You're probably still holding your breath waiting to hear why the most famous case in Torts history is bogus.[27] *Because it never happened*, at least not the way people think it did. The illustrious *Prosser* casebook even tells us this in a note following the case:

> [T]he event could not have possibly happened. These were apparently ordinary fireworks, and not bombs.… [They fell] in the pit below the edge of the platform, which would have protected the scale. No one testified to seeing it fall over.… Plaintiff's original complaint … alleged that the scale was knocked over by a stampede of frightened passengers. If that is what happened, would Judge Cardozo allow Mrs. Palsgraf to recover for her injuries? Would Judge Andrews?[28]

Understandably, a student's first response upon reading this note is: "If the freaking book says the case didn't really happen, why are we spending two weeks talking about it?" The instinctive second response is to try to answer the two questions at the end of the note about Cardozo and Andrews. As covered in Chapter 1, the correct answers are, respectively: "Beats the heck out of me" and "Beats the heck out of me."

How did an accident that never happened become the most famous case in Torts history? The answer lies in this little-known transcript of an in-chambers colloquy between Cardozo and Andrews:

---

[27] If you are, that's pretty impressive and you should consider becoming a pearl diver instead of a lawyer.

[28] PROSSER ET AL, TORTS: CASES AND MATERIALS 311 n.2 (10th ed. 2000).

Cardozo: This is the most ridiculous case I've ever seen. There's only one answer.

Andrews: Dismiss it?

Cardozo: No way. Let's write legendary exceedingly complex opinions about it. Remember back in law school how everybody hated us because we were always raising our hands with the right answers? Here's our chance to get even. Picture all those law students obsessing about a legendary case that never happened. Imagine the panic attacks. It's rich!

Andrews: It does sound fun, but what makes you think this preposterous mess will become legendary?

Cardozo: Look, I'm a big name. People think everything I write is legendary. Here, I'm going to say a person is liable for negligence only if the plaintiff was foreseeable.

Andrews: What's so legendary about that?

Cardozo: The *way* I'm going to say it. I'm going to obfuscate the hell out of it. Obfuscation is the key to all great opinions. Just look at *Pennoyer v. Neff*. Here's a sample I already drafted: "What the plaintiff must show is a wrong to herself; i.e., a violation of her own right, and not merely a wrong to someone else, nor

conduct wrongful because unsocial, but not a wrong to anyone."

Andrews: What the hell does that mean?

Cardozo: Nothing! That's the beauty of it. It gets even better: "Negligence, like risk, is thus a term of relation. Negligence in the abstract, apart from things related, is surely not a tort, if indeed it is understandable at all."

Andrews: I don't understand that at all, but I guess that's the point. What should my legendary opinion say?

Cardozo: Let's really mess with their heads by writing about two completely different subjects. I'll go on and on about duty, then just when they think they might be figuring things out, you start talking about proximate cause. Use that ridiculous hypo you're so fond of.

Andrews: The chauffeur and the car full of dynamite? That's no hypo. It's a joke. The chauffeur says to the guy with the dyna—

Cardozo: Whatever. Just cram it in there somehow. And remember—the overriding goal is to write an opinion that makes the reader think he's losing his mind.

Hopefully, this insight will help you set your goals more realistically when reading *Palsgraf*. Don't even think about

trying to understand it. Consider it a major triumph if you make it through the whole opinion without passing out.

Contracts: *Hadley v. Baxendale,*
9 Exch. 341 (Court of Exchequer 1854)

Hadley v. Baxendale is the granddaddy of Contracts cases, a relic from the English Court of Exchequer that every first-year law student is required to master. It stands for the important principle that damages for breach of contract are limited to what the parties could reasonably foresee at the time of contracting. Basically, the case says that if the foreseeable results of a breach of contract are A, B and C, you cannot be held legally responsible for X, Y and Z, at least not if you make it to Costa Rica before the court acquires personal jurisdiction of you.

Hadley doesn't suffer from the same flaws as *Palsgraf*, but has a defect of its own, which is that it's one of the most boring things ever written.

Hadley hired Baxendale to transport a broken mill shaft for repair. Because Hadley's mill couldn't operate without the shaft, time was of the essence. Baxendale transported the shaft to Greenwich for repair by canal and it arrived late, causing Hadley to lose business. Hadley sued for lost revenues, but couldn't recover them because—this is the key fact—he hadn't informed Baxendale of his special circumstances. Because Hadley didn't tell Baxendale that his mill couldn't operate without the shaft, his lost profits were viewed as an unforeseeable consequence of the contract breach.

Here's how the English court described the exciting action:

> [A]t the last Gloucester Assizes, it appeared that the plaintiffs carried on an extensive business as millers at Gloucester; and that, on the 11th of May, their mill was stopped by a breakage of the crank shaft by which the mill was worked....[29]

From a reader interest standpoint, this introduction suffers from several flaws, not the least of which is that people hate sentences with "assizes" in them. I fear *Hadley* risks losing its classic status because it's such a snoozer. Law schools need to keep in step with the times. I propose that someone with a lot of money, possibly the federal government or Wal-Mart®, hire John Grisham to rewrite *Hadley* with a view toward making it more interesting, more comprehensible and possibly into a blockbuster movie. Here's an example of what a little punching up can do for this antique:

> *Shark attack!* Baxendale watches in shock as the Great White, rare in English canals, rises from the dank water and devours the front of his boat.
>
> He hadn't counted on this. "Now I'll be late delivering the mill shaft for sure." Hefting the broken shaft as a harpoon, he dives in the canal to fight the shark, oblivious to the men in the black sedan parked on the barge following him.
>
> Meanwhile …

---

[29] 9 Exch. at 344.

Hadley pulls from Rita's embrace. "I need time to think," he says sullenly and retreats to the veranda with his glass of whiskey. Where was Baxendale? The fool was two days late arriving at Greenwich with the broken shaft. Everything depended on that shaft getting fixed on time. His career, the mill, his dark secret ... Rita.

He feels her silky touch and turns to accept her waiting lips, all the while thinking: *I should have told Baxendale this delivery was important, but I forgot.*

Meanwhile ...

Baxendale stumbles into the repair shop and collapses. Three days late, but it's a miracle he made it at all. He had to drag the Great White twenty miles—on one leg—after it swallowed the mill shaft. Why had he done it? For 2£, 4 s., and he wasn't even sure how much money that was. Yet he risked his life. Risked everything ... for Rita.

Peppier than the original, don't you agree? Think of all the benefits. The updated version would help keep students from falling into comas while reading it, make for livelier class discussion and could generate millions in movie and merchandising rights. People would be lined up outside McDonald's® to get little Hadley, Baxendale and especially Rita action figures in their Happy Meals®©©. Unfortunately, unless and until law schools show the vision to move forward into the modern era, you'll be stuck with the old version, assizes and all.

Civil Procedure: *Pennoyer v. Neff*
95 U.S. 714 (U.S. Supreme Court 1877)

Pennoyer v. Neff. Pennoyer v. Neff. Pennoyer v. Neff. Pennoyer v. Neff. Pennoyer v. Neff. Pennoyer v. Neff. Pennoyer v. Neff. Pennoyer v. Neff. Pennoyer v. Neff. Glennoyer v. Feff.[30] Pennoyer v. Neff. Pennoyer v. Neff.

Mostly, what lawyers remember about *Pennoyer v. Neff* is the name. They would like to remember more, such as what the case was about, but since they never understood it, that's impossible. This is not a case of a memory being bumped from the brain by a more important memory as discussed at the beginning of the chapter. This is a situation where a memory is never in contention to be remembered in the first place because it lacks a sufficient foundation.

In an amazing discovery, scientists recently identified a gland at the entrance to the human memory that acts like a bouncer in a bar, checking the credentials of every memory that tries to get in. In law school, with some frequency, vague, stupefied thoughts masquerading as memories seek to enter. The gland's job is to send them packing.

Our very expensive computerized magnetic resonance imaging process allows us to see exactly how the average law student's limited understanding of *Pennoyer v. Neff* works to disqualify the case as a viable memory:

---

[30] Just making sure you're paying attention.

Bouncer Gland: Hold it. Identify yourself.

P v. N Memory: Pennoyer v. Neff.

Gland: And what, pray tell, is a Pennoyer v. Neff?

Memory: Pennoyer v. Neff.

Gland: Circumstances of memory?

Memory: Pennoyer v. Neff.

Gland: Witnesses to the alleged memory?

Memory: Pennoyer, Neff.

Gland: Emotions experienced when memory incurred?

Memory: Pennoyerism, neffistration.

Gland: Comprehension level?

Memory: Pennoyer v. Neff.

Gland: I'm sorry. You don't qualify as a memory. You can't come in here. But have a nice day.

Memory: Pennoyer v. Neff.

Some lawyers do remember that *Pennoyer v. Neff* has to do with the complicated issue of personal jurisdiction. To sue someone, the court where the lawsuit is filed must have "personal jurisdiction" of the defendant. In *Pennoyer*, the Supreme Court basically said this can occur only where either the defendant or his property is present in the forum state. Like many classic cases that are analyzed endlessly in law school, *Pennoyer* has little modern relevance, as the law

of personal jurisdiction has changed dramatically.

To sue an out-of-state defendant, it's no longer necessary that defendants be present in the state, but only that they have what are called "minimum contacts" with the state. The rules for what constitute sufficient minimum contacts are being considerably loosened as courts take heed of the frightening fact that citizens are running out of people to sue in their own states. Today, the minimum contacts rule can be satisfied by extremely minor contacts with the forum state. One court recently ruled that minimum contacts exist if the defendant makes a mildly amusing remark anywhere within the U.S., on the theory that some person with no life will convert the remark into a humorous forwarded e-mail, which, like all humorous forwarded e-mail, will end up clogging the computer of every resident domiciled in all 50 states.

As you probably noticed, *Pennoyer* also suffers from the *Hadley* problem. It's boring. However, the colorful background of the plaintiff in the case, a Portland lawyer named J.H. Mitchell, helps make up for it. You're probably hoping I'll explain to you why the case isn't called *Mitchell v. Neff* since Mitchell and not Pennoyer was the plaintiff. This is just another one of those hilarious pranks the law plays on law students. You can never rely on the case name to tell you who the main players are. A case called *Smith v. Jones* may very well be about two guys named Romanowski.

In any event, HERE'S SOMETHING REALLY INTEREST-ING ABOUT THE FAMOUSLY TEDIOUS *PENNOYER V. NEFF*: The plaintiff, J.H. Mitchell, started out as a school-teacher in Pennsylvania, where he seduced a 15-year-old

girl, was forced to marry her, left teaching and took up law, headed west in 1860, established himself as a successful lawyer, got married again without bothering to divorce his first wife, sued Neff, GOT ELECTED TO THE U.S. SENATE in 1872, was scandalized when the trial judge in *Pennoyer v. Neff* came into possession of love letters Mitchell had sent to his second wife's younger sister with whom he was having a five-year affair and GOT RE-ELECTED TO THE U.S. SENATE four days after the letters were published in the newspaper.[31]

So one lesson to be learned from *Pennoyer* is that while the law may sometimes be boring, lawyers can be very exciting.

Property: *Jee v. Audley*
1 Cox 324, 39 Eng. Rep. 116 (Court of Chancery 1787)

One of the great perversions of legal education is the amount of time and energy students are forced to expend mastering an arcane area of property law known as "future interests." First-semester law students devote hundreds of hours to figuring out future interests, even though only one out of a thousand lawyers will ever use them in real life. In the 20 years since I graduated from law school, I have never even seen the words "future interest" except on a tarot card reader's sign asking "Does the future interest you? Madame Borg can answer all your questions."

---

[31] Documented in Wendy Perdue, *Sin, Scandal and Substantive Due Process*, 62 WASHINGTON LAW REVIEW 479, 481-90 (1987).

What are future interests? I asked Madame Borg, but she only gave me her prediction that I would never need to know. So I got out my old Property notes, but that was a mistake because it triggered post-traumatic stress flashbacks similar to those suffered by Vietnam veterans and LSD users who have bad trips. My own flashback was a particularly horrific combination of the two. I was sitting in a Property class of Viet Cong soldiers analyzing future interests to the tune of *Purple Haze* with the Tet Offensive raging outside. Jimi Hendrix was the professor, but since he was speaking Vietnamese, he sounded exactly like my real Property professor. Frankly, it was a terrifying experience, although it was pretty cool when Professor Hendrix set his casebook on fire.

Then it all came flooding back. Future interests are future ownership rights to land created by a landowner in a will or a trust. They're the ultimate weapon for control freaks because they allow property owners to say who can use their property in what ways long after they're dead.

How long? The answer lies in the Rule Against Perpetuities, which has already been discussed as a major source of grief for law students. In the interest of not provoking my loyal readers to stalk and murder me, I won't attempt to explain the RAP again. Suffice it to say that *Jee v. Audley* established one of the great doctrines from the Rule Against Perpetuities known as the "fertile octogenarian rule."

Of course, anything having to do with "fertile octogenarians" must be funny. You can easily test this theory by gathering any group of highly-serious senior law partners in a conference room. The more dour the

partners, the better the test results. First, get them in a really bad mood by telling them insurance costs are skyrocketing, the copiers are harassing the fax machines and the staff is threatening to strike unless Casual Day is expanded to include Pajama Week and Beach Party Summer. Administer the test by reading explanations of the Rule Against Perpetuities from any standard hornbook. By the time you get to the part about fertile octogenarians, the partners will be flipping each other's ties, snorting milk out their noses and making funny sounds with their armpits.

The fertile octogenarian rule is a binding legal presumption that any person—no matter how old—can bear a child. Eighty years old? No problem. Might as well start stocking up on Pampers®. Ninety? Invite any living friends to a baby shower. A hundred years old, no ovaries, live in a padlocked iron lung? Doesn't matter. The rule says it's possible for you to have children.

Needless to say, the rule is based on antiquated legal presumptions rather than hard science. Experiments show that spermatozoa, although quite sneaky, do not know how to pick padlocks.

Criminal Law: *Regina v. Dudley*
14 Q.B.D. 273 (Queen's Bench 1884)

Finally, a case you can sink your teeth into. This is the tale of some castaways who, after being stranded on a lifeboat for 20 days with nothing to eat but two cans of turnips and a turtle, cannabalized a 17-year-old cabin boy. Four days

later they were rescued by a passing ship. Oops!

Back in England, the three survivors faced a variety of criminal charges, including Assault With a Deadly Molar and Abdominal Possession of a Fibula. Also murder. The crewmen defended on the ground of "justification." The defense of justification says you can commit a crime without penalty so long as it is committed in the interest of avoiding a greater harm. For example, one would be legally "justified" in trespassing and breaking and entering if that was the only way to avoid running into Geraldo Rivera.

In *Regina v. Dudley*, the defendants argued it was better that one cabin boy should die than that all of them starve, which isn't a bad argument if you think about it. After all, the jury specifically found:

> **[A]t the time of the act in question there was no sail in sight, nor any reasonable prospect of relief, not even a Starbucks® [32].... [U]nder these circumstances there appeared to the prisoners every probability that unless they then fed or very soon fed upon the boy or one of themselves they would die of starvation.[33]**

But oops again. The defendants never consulted the cabin boy for his thoughts on the matter before slitting his throat and feasting on his flesh.

The jurors rejected the justification defense and sentenced the defendants to death. Interviewed after the

---

[32] Kidding about the Starbucks®.
[33] 14 Q.B.D. at 275.

verdict, one juror said he simply could not condone such an uncivilized act, adding he would have voted differently had the cabin boy been cooked *al dente* and served with a decent merlot.

However, the English Crown commuted the death sentence to only six months imprisonment, thereby implicitly accepting the justification defense. After all, six months is a light sentence even in today's tolerant society. In most states, you have to serve at least a year for slitting a person's throat and devouring him, unless you're a juvenile, in which case your Gameboy® privileges can be revoked for up to six months in states with tough juvenile sentencing laws.

The defense of justification is rarely raised in criminal cases, which I think is a mistake because, let's face it, there's something pretty great about a legal defense that lets you commit any crime if you can think of a good enough reason. However, the justification defense is frequently invoked *unofficially*. This happens in murder cases where the defendant's lawyer pursues what is known as the "deserved to die" defense. For real. In situations where your murder client is guilty as sin, but had the good fortune or judgment to kill a real S.O.B., a common defense strategy is to subtly persuade the jury that the victim got what he deserved.

Consider the recent murder trial of Francine Flogwocker, accused of killing her husband with an ax. The state's case was strong. The prosecution had the ax dripping with the defendant's DNA and this damaging 911 recording:

911 Operator:	911. What's the problem?
Defendant:	My husband's been attacked with an ax.
911 Operator:	Is he breathing?
Defendant:	More like snoring. The man can't even die without displaying his disgusting habits.
911 Operator:	We'll be there in five minutes.
Defendant:	Hurry. Five minutes with this cretin is a lifetime.

Faced with overwhelming evidence of guilt, defense counsel relied on the defense of justification, presenting evidence that in the days leading up to the offense the victim forgot their wedding anniversary, told defendant she looked like she was gaining weight, acted like he deserved recognition as Father of the Year for grudgingly driving the kids to soccer practice for the first time in his life, sat on the couch for 72 straight hours flipping channels, and, immediately preceding the 153 ax blows, accused defendant of having a bad attitude, adding "it must be that time of the month."

The all-women jury not only acquitted the defendant, but stopped on the way home and bought their own axes.

Five memorable cases, five thousand bottles of Tylenol®. The most amazing thing about these cases is that they're all irrelevant to the practice of law. You will never see them discussed in legal pleadings. A lawyer citing *Palsgraf* would be laughed out of court. But we love and cherish them anyway. Why? The same reason classic rock stations continue to play songs by Bachman Turner Overdrive with alarming frequency. When you grow up with something, it becomes part of you, even if it sucks. And one thing is for sure: for better or worse, you definitely grow up in law school.

10
LEGAL
RESEARCH
& WRITING

egal Research and Writing doesn't have any famous cases, but deserves its own chapter because it's the most important course in law school and also because that last chapter was getting way too long.

All law schools require first-year students to take Legal Research and Writing, a highly labor-intensive course. Usually, the workload for a law school course corresponds to the number of credit hours for the course. The more credit hours allotted, the more work required. But we reversed everything for Legal Research and Writing. We require a lot more work than other courses for fewer credit hours.

In this single course, a student is expected to master legal research, understand the bizarre *Bluebook*, compose at least two sophisticated legal memoranda and, in the second semester, write an appellate brief and present an oral argument to a panel of judges. Students are sometimes overheard complaining that allotting only two credit hours for legal writing is arbitrary and capricious. This is not correct. Everything is done according to a scientific, mathematical formula:

$$\frac{x}{y} = 2 \textbf{ credit hours}$$

with *x* being the number of hours required to master Legal

Research and Writing (rounded off to the nearest thousand) and y being the number necessary to make the answer equal 2 credit hours.

Leegle Righting

Be kind to your legal writing instructors. They have the hardest job in legal education. Forget *legal* writing. Legal writing instructors are forced to spend long hours working with students who never learned regular writing. Take a look at this Torts exam written many years ago by a student at a law school in the Midwest. The student was asked to analyze a hypothetical tortious situation involving a dog-bite injury and subsequent trespass.

> **I SEe DAwG. DAwG choo A's leg. See A run. A run to B's howse. B get mad and soo. A soo too. He soo DAwg. A loose. B win mony.**

Pitiful, even if Dan Quayle did go on to become vice-president.[34]

---

[34] You may say, "Why pick on Dan Quayle?" Because when he addressed the United Negro College Fund in 1989, in an apparent attempt to capitalize on the organization's slogan that "A mind is a terrible thing to waste," he said: "What a waste it is to lose one's mind— or to not have a mind. How true that is." Want another reason? Because in responding to an inquiry about how he could help the Republican party carry California in 1992, he said: "I love California; I grew up in Phoenix." More? Okay, because in commenting in 1988 on his response to the Vietnam War, he said: "I do, I do, I do, I do what any normal person would do at that age. You call home. You call home to mother and father and say, 'I'd like to get in the National Guard.'" These and many other "Quayludes" are contained in a book by David Oliver called *Political Babble: The 1,000 Dumbest Things Ever Said by Politicians.*

Whereases, Wherefores and Other Whegal Whubbish

Even students with good writing skills present challenges for legal writing instructors. Students come to law school thinking legal writing is all *whereases, wherefores* and other convoluted jargon, when, in fact, good legal writing is like any other good writing: clear and terse. First-year law students, intoxicated by the law, insist on making everything in their lives overly legalistic. Check out this note I intercepted being passed in class:

> Whereas the party of the first part has been requested by the party of the second part to participate in a joint venture on the evening of Friday, October 15, and whereas in consideration of the party of the first part's assent to this agreement the party of the second part agrees to fully capitalize said joint venture, the party of the first part hereby covenants to go to a movie.
>
> Whereas the party of the first part hates missing the previews of coming attractions and would never consider going on a second joint venture with someone who showed up late, it is understood that time is of the essence in the performance of this contract.
>
> Physical contact during the period of said joint venture is strictly prohibited, including but not limited to hugging, squeezing, hand-holding, knee-patting, elbow-brushing, goodnight-kissing

or fondling of any kind. The party of the second part assumes the risk of getting maced if he even thinks about violating this paragraph.

This agreement is subject to cancellation without notice if the party of the first part gets a better offer.

Wherefore Art Thou, Adjectives?

And then there are the students—usually former English and Fine Arts students—who go to the opposite extreme. Feeling stifled by the conventions of legal writing, they want to turn everything into a literary masterpiece. Schooled in the works of Shakespeare and Faulkner, these students sometimes find it hard to accept that good legal writing is sparse, almost devoid of adjectives and stylish prose.

A Criminal Law exam once asked this straightforward essay question concerning homicidal intent:

Criminal Law: Essay Question

A buys a jar of rat poison. She writes in her diary that she wishes to use the poison to kill B, her husband. The next morning, A changes her mind and throws the poison out the window. B is walking outside. The bottle strikes B on the head and kills him. Did A have the requisite mental intent for the crime of homicide?

Here's the answer turned in by a former Creative Writing student:

Criminal Law: Answer to Essay Question

"B! Wake thee! Oh, I do beseech thee to breathe," A said, caressing B's gaping cranium in her lithe arms. B's cerebellum seeped in lazy curly-cues down his bluish cheek, soaking the gossamer threads of her nightgown in crimson pools.

The bottle of rat poison mocked her from its resting place inside B's skull, the vermin on the label posed as if it intended to leap into what little brain matter remained to gnaw its way to B's innermost thoughts.

"Oh, woe and more woe. Thoughts black. Deeds deep. Twas just last evening I prayed for B's demise—yet I altered my wishes before the bitter bird of arsenic took its sanguinary swan dive. Surely the law could not condemn one for the feelings of ill will so natural to the married state."

But she knew she could not risk prison. Better death at her own hand than even five seconds of precious liberty ripped from her alabaster bosom.

In the distance, through the glass-spun web of fog and the ticking clock of the Criminal Law exam, police sirens wailed, demon curses chasing one another into the dank night.

The sirens drew closer. Desolation. Isolation. Attorney's fees. A woeful bummer. "Oh, woe, woe, woe, woe, woe," A said, ripping the poison

from its nest of ooze.

As she imbibed, she waxed whimsically about the important legal doctrine of intent. "'Tis like love itself," she sighed. "Unable to grasp and it changes really fast." She laid back and closed her eyes, at peace with the harmony of law and love.

The infinite souls who've given more than passing thought to abrogating thy significant other shall weep at the grave of this brave, innocent woman.

THE END

© 2001 Exam No. 689 All Rights Reserved.

A lucky few of these poetic souls go on to become judges and, because judges can do anything they want, find an outlet for their creativity. In *Fisher v. Lowe*, the plaintiff sued defendant for driving his automobile into plaintiff's oak tree, damaging the tree. The Michigan trial court ruled in favor of the defendant and the Court of Appeals affirmed. Here is the court's actual opinion:

> *We thought that we would never see*
> *A suit to compensate a tree.*
> *A suit whose claim in tort is prest*
> *Upon a mangled tree's behest;*
> *A tree whose battered trunk was prest*
> *Against a Chevy's crumpled crest;*
> *A tree that faces each new day*
> *With bark and limb in disarray;*
> *A tree that may forever bear*

A lasting need for tender care.
Flora lovers though we three,
We must uphold the court's decree.
Affirmed.[35]

Getting Anal About the Oral Argument

Ask law students to list five classic terror-fests and you're likely to get:

1. *Scream*
2. *Nightmare on Elm Street*
3. *Halloween*
4. *Psycho*
5. *The Oral Argument*

In the second semester at most law schools, you will be given a fictional case and assigned to represent one of the parties in an appeal. You will do months of research and prepare a lengthy written brief arguing your appeal. Preparation of the brief is difficult and time-consuming, but it gets much worse. After submitting the brief, you have to get up in front of a panel of three judges and argue the case. This "oral argument," as it is known, is the scariest event of the first year.

Surveys show public speaking to be the number one fear of most Americans. Death comes in second and picking the

---

[35] *Fisher v. Lowe*, 112 Mich. App. 418, 333 N.W. 2d 67 (Court of Appeals of Michigan 1983).

slowest checkout lane at the supermarket third. An appellate argument is public speaking at its most terrifying because you can't rely on memorizing or reading prepared remarks. Lawyers are lucky to get out even one complete sentence in oral argument before being peppered with questions by the judges.

Of course, this doesn't stop law students from writing out their entire oral argument word for word and memorizing it forwards, backwards, every other word, vowels only, in different languages and put to music. Who can blame them? I did the same thing. Not many people are courageous enough to attempt a public presentation without writing it out first. But it's all for naught.

Our first-year students were assigned an interesting appellate problem involving a defendant who sold research papers to college students over the Internet. A fictional university, whose students were buying the papers and submitting them for course work, filed a lawsuit for fraud and obtained an injunction. Defendant appealed the injunction, claiming his business activity was protected free speech under the first amendment.

It was exciting to watch the students burn the midnight oil in the law library as they prepared for their oral arguments, although it got a little scary when they ran out of midnight oil and set fire to the Federal Supplement. As usual, most students wrote out their arguments and memorized them verbatim. But also as usual, this proved to be wasted effort. Here's a transcript from an oral argument presented by a student representing the plaintiff/appellee university:

Student:	May it please the court, my name is—
Judge No. 1:	Aren't these research papers protected speech under the first amend-ment? Suppose I want to buy one of the appellant's research papers for my own edification. Shouldn't I have the right to do that?
Student:	I—
Judge No. 2:	Where is the requisite "irreparable harm" necessary for a preliminary injunction? I don't see that here at all.
Student:	It—
Judge No. 3:	I'm having a hard time with your fraud claim. The plagiarizing students seem to be the ones committing the fraud. All the appellant is doing is selling research papers. How can that constitute fraud?
Student:	Well—
Judge No. 1:	Thank you, counselor. We've heard enough. Sit down.

This is good news. It means you can cut way down on your preparation time and save paper too. Forget writing out the whole argument. Simply jot down "I," "It" and "Well" on a Post-It® note and you'll have all you need.

s a law student, it's important to be conversant about topical legal issues. Your friends and family will expect this of you. Everywhere you go—cocktail parties, neighborhood barbecues, crack houses—people will have legal questions.

Studies show Americans have an average of five legal problems at any given moment. Studies also show that people like to get things of value without having to pay for them. The combined results of these studies mean that all your friends, relatives and acquaintances will want free legal advice from you. And beginning on your first day of law school, they will expect you to know the answer to every possible legal question in every possible area of law—criminal law, contract law, tort law, property law, business law, environmental law, tax law, antitrust law, patent law, securities law, international law and especially, intellectual property law—off the top of your head. When you don't know the answer— and you never will—they will shake their heads in disappointment and look at you suspiciously. Don't feel bad. Even the smartest, most experienced lawyers have to research most legal questions to find reliable answers. The only legal question you absolutely must know the answer to is "Where is the law library?"

But it is important to SOUND knowledgeable about the law, particularly about topical legal issues likely to arise in cocktail chatter. Even superficial familiarity with a topic

can carry you a long way in conversation with laypersons. With that goal in mind, here is a primer on four of the hottest legal issues in America.

Products Liability

Tort liability for defective products may be the most controversial legal issue in all of law. Products liability is the body of law that allows people who have been injured by a "defective product" to recover money from the manufacturer. Well-known defective products include Ford Pintos and asbestos. On the other hand, Ford Pintos made of asbestos probably would have been a good idea.

The most volatile area of the products liability law dispute involves liability for defective warnings on products. Here's one area where the critics have a legitimate point. The law requires product manufacturers to warn of potential dangers posed by their products. If an adequate warning is omitted, the product is considered legally "defective" and the manufacturer has to pay damages.

To avoid the risk that a jury may later declare a warning to be inadequate, corporate legal departments have gone crazy plastering warnings about anything and everything on all our products. Of course, this only guarantees we won't read any of them. Here are a dozen AUTHENTIC silly warnings,[36] along with my absolutely free legal advice for improving them:

---

[36] I thank my students at the University of Arkansas at Little Rock for providing me with most of these warnings on "Stupid Warnings Day" in my Products Liability course. These warning label excerpts were collected over a period of years and may not be current.

ACTUAL AIRBAG WARNING IN OWNER'S MANUAL FOR JEEP CHEROKEE®

WARNING: Being too close to the steering wheel or instrument panel during airbag deployment could cause serious injury. Airbags need room to inflate. Sit back, comfortably extending your arms to reach the steering wheel or instrument panel.

MCCLURG'S SUGGESTED ADDITION

Obviously, to follow this warning, it is essential that you plan all accidents in advance. Since airbags inflate most safely when no one is in the car, we recommend parking and exiting your vehicle prior to any accident.

ACTUAL WARNINGS ACCOMPANYING A SKIL® CORDLESS SCREWDRIVER

WARNING: Keep work area well lit.... Do not let visitors contact tool .... All visitors should be kept away from the work area.... DRESS PROPERLY. Do not wear loose clothing or jewelry. They can be caught in moving parts. Rubber gloves and non-skid footwear are recommended when working outdoors. Wear protective hair covering to contain long hair.... STAY ALERT. Watch what you are doing. Use common sense. Do not operate tool when you are tired.... DON'T OVERREACH. Keep proper footing and balance at all times.

MCCLURG'S SUGGESTED ADDITION

Always wear a welding mask and flame-retardant suit approved by NASCAR when operating a cordless screwdriver. Have a team of expert engineers, general contractors, physicians, faith healers and lawyers standing by in case of trouble. Keep an ambulance idling in the driveway at all times. DO NOT OPERATE A CORDLESS SCREW-DRIVER EXCEPT WHILE ON PHONE WITH A 911 DISPATCHER. If possible, try to be in another state when the screwdriver is actually switched on.

ACTUAL WARNING ON SENSORPACK® CARBON MONOXIDE DETECTOR

WARNING: Carbon monoxide detectors are not a substitute for life insurance. Though these detectors warn against increasing CO levels, we do not warrant or imply in any way that they will protect lives from CO poisoning. Homeowners and renters must still insure their lives.

MCCLURG'S SUGGESTED ADDITION

You may be asking yourself, "Why waste money on a carbon monoxide detector that the manufacturer does 'not imply in any way' will protect you from carbon monoxide poisoning?" It's a good question, but you'd have to talk to our legal department to get the answer. If you'll just buy the life insurance like we suggest, you can quit worrying about it. "Wait a

second. Did I read that right?" "Yeah, that's what the lawyers said to put in there." "Life insurance?" "That's what they told me." "That's the most ridiculous thing I've ever heard." "I know, but—hold it—the secretary's still taking dictation. Hey! Stop typing."

ACTUAL WARNING ON SILLY PUTTY®

WARNING: Not intended for use as ear plugs.

MCCLURG'S SUGGESTED ADDITION

Also not intended for use as chewing gum, gymnastics mat, contraceptive diaphragm, submarine leak repair kit, optical lens, cat toy, spare tire, breakfast biscuit or anything else. Truth is, this product has no intended purpose, which makes it pretty funny that we've sold more than 500 billion packages of the stuff.

ACTUAL WARNING ON WINCHESTER BLACK TALON® AMMUNITION

LEAD WARNING: Discharging ammunition in poorly ventilated areas ... or handling ammunition may result in exposure to lead, a substance known to cause birth defects, reproductive harm, and other serious physical injury.... Wash hands thoroughly after exposure.

MCCLURG'S SUGGESTED ADDITION

Exposure to the lead in this product may also result in gaping chest wounds. Wash wounds thoroughly after exposure.

ACTUAL WARNING ON FRISBEE®
FLEXIBLE FLYING DISC FOR DOGS

WARNING: THIS IS A DOG TOY. IT IS NOT A THERAPEUTIC DEVICE ... DO NOT THROW IT DIRECTLY AT YOUR DOG.

MCCLURG'S SUGGESTED ADDITION

If you do, your dog will likely experience feelings of rejection and anxiety and require therapy, but, as we just told you, this is not a therapeutic device and most HMOs do not provide adequate mental health coverage for pets.

ACTUAL WARNING ON REVLON®
HAND-HELD HAIR BLOWER

WARNING: Never use while sleeping.

MCCLURG'S SUGGESTED ADDITION

If you do not understand why, immediately return this and every other product you own to place of purchase.

ACTUAL WARNING ON UNITED AIRLINES® B-727 SAFETY CARD

WARNING: If you are sitting in an exit row and you cannot read this card … please tell a crew member.

MCCLURG'S SUGGESTED ADDITION

If you really can't read this card, allow us to also tell you how much we hate it when you idiots ignore the carry-on baggage rules, never have correct change for drinks and wait to go to the bathroom until we've got the serving cart stuck in the middle of the aisle.

ACTUAL WARNING ON NINTENDO GAMEBOY® HAND-HELD VIDEO GAME PLAYER

WARNING: Some people may experience fatigue or discomfort after playing for a long time. Regardless of how you feel, you should ALWAYS take a 10 to 15 minute break every hour while playing. If your hands or arms become tired or uncomfortable while playing, stop and rest. If you continue to experience soreness or discomfort during or after play, listen to the signals your body is giving you. Stop playing and consult a doctor.

MCCLURG'S SUGGESTED ADDITION

We realize no kid in the history of the universe has ever read a product warning. We also know it's absurd to think a kid is going to time his Nintendo

playing and take 10 to 15 minute breaks every hour. The part about listening to your body's signals and stopping play to consult a doctor had us rolling on the floor. But even a little sport like yourself has probably figured out that the main purpose of product warnings is to protect manufacturers from lawsuits.

ACTUAL WARNING ON TRU-TURN® FISH HOOK PACKAGE

WARNING: All fish hooks are inherently dangerous!

MCCLURG'S SUGGESTED ADDITION

Years of study have finally disclosed the cause: they're pointy. We tried making them without points, but the fish started stealing them and using them to hang coffee mugs on.

ACTUAL WARNING ON ANGELIC VISIONS® INCENSE THAT TOUTS MAGICAL PROPERTIES SUCH AS ECSTASY AND MYSTIC KNOWLEDGE

Sold as curio only, no magical effects are guaranteed.

MCCLURG'S SUGGESTED ADDITION

If you do experience magical effects, it's probably not from the incense, but from that other product you're using the incense to cover up.

ACTUAL WARNING ON GENERAL ELECTRIC
"WALT DISNEY'S MICKEY MOUSE NITE LITE®"[37]

CAUTION: This is not a toy and is not intended for use by children.

MCCLURG'S SUGGESTED ADDITION

Kids, if you're ever tempted to think a Mickey Mouse product is intended for use by children, simply call our toll free number and one of our intellectual property lawyers will send you to Time Out.

The Supreme Court

The United States Supreme Court is the most powerful judicial tribunal in the world. It has the last say on every important decision in America. The Court can overrule Congress, the President and even the instant replay officials at NFL football games. The all-powerful Supreme Court is a body that every American citizen needs to know about, especially law students. To converse intelligently about the Supreme Court, law students need to know four things: the justices' names, their legal philosophies, their voting patterns and how to pronounce the word "certiorari."

1. The Justices' Names. Law students need to learn the names of the nine Supreme Court justices. Why? Because it

---

[37] Honestly, I have no idea whether these are all registered trademarks, but I'm not taking any chances.

sounds bad when you're trying to carry on an intellectual discussion about Supreme Court jurisprudence and you keep referring to Chief Justice William Rehnquist as the "head dude" or Justice Ruth Bader Ginsburg as "the chick with the bun in her hair." In alphabetical order, here are the nine current justices of the U.S. Supreme Court: Tyra Banks, Sandra Bullock, Cindy Crawford, Nicole Kidman, Anna Kournikova, Jennifer Lopez, Chief Justice Tina Turner and Shania Twain.

Sorry. Wrong list. That's my wish list of people I want to be on the Supreme Court if I ever end up stranded with the Supreme Court on a desert island. Here's the real lineup: Stephen "Delete Footnote? Yes." Breyer,[38] Sandra Day "MC Sandy D" O'Connor, Ruth Bader "I'm Short But I Can Dunk" Ginsburg, Anthony "No, Not Those Kennedys" Kennedy, Chief Justice William "Billy, Don't Be a Hero" Rehnquist, Antonin "Nino the Great" Scalia, John Paul "Why Did My Parents Give Me Two First Names?" Stevens, David "The Quiet Beatle" Souter and Clarence "Mr. Excitement" Thomas.

2. Their Legal Philosophies. The most important part of a Supreme Court justice's job is interpreting the Constitution. There are two major competing legal philosophies for how to go about doing this. The first one is known as "strict constructionism." Strict

---

[38] Justice Breyer is well-known for his aversion to footnotes. In an interview published in *The Docket Sheet*, the Court's employee newsletter, Breyer explained why he shuns footnotes: "[E]ither a point is sufficiently significant to make, in which case it should be in the text, or it is not, in which case, don't make it."

constructionists interpret the Constitution by focusing on the plain meaning of the actual words. They criticize followers of the other philosophy, known as "judicial activism," or "Let's do whatever the hell we want because we're not accountable to anyone-ism." The strict constructionists accuse judicial activists of interpreting the Constitution to promote their own views of what is good, regardless of whether their results are supported by language in the Constitution.

However, contrary to popular belief, there is not really much difference between strict constructionists and judicial activists. Both types of justices are devoutly dedicated to following the Constitution except in cases where it would lead to results they don't like. Because most constitutional provisions are written in vague, broad language, both approaches allow justices considerable leeway for result-oriented decision making. The major difference in the approaches is how they are applied.

For example, suppose the Court was faced with the appeal of an army private convicted of hacksawing his company commander into four pieces during a dispute in the defendant's barracks over whether defendant was being all that he could be. Both strict constructionists and judicial activists would want to uphold the conviction for such a heinous crime, even if they believed the defendant's constitutional rights were violated, but they would go about it in different ways.

The strict constructionists would want to find specific language in the Constitution to pin their decision on. They most likely would rely on the often-overlooked

Third Amendment, which states:

Amendment III
No Soldier shall, in time of peace be quartered in any house, without the consent of the owner, nor in time of war, but in a manner prescribed by law.

Strict constructionists would reason that since the major was cut into four pieces, he was technically "quartered" within the meaning of the amendment. Moreover, the defendant did not have "the consent of the owner" of the barracks—the U.S. government—to hacksaw superior officers. To the contrary, the U.S. would assert that NOT hacksawing superior officers was an implied condition of residing on the property. Finally, after consulting CNN, the strict constructionists would take judicial notice that the nation is not at war. All conditions of the Third Amendment being satisfied, the justices would vote to uphold defendant's conviction. Judicial activists would arrive at the same result, but use divergent reasoning. They would reason, "Defendant loses because we believe it is good."

3. Their Voting Patterns. Understanding Supreme Court voting patterns is a difficult challenge because the nine justices rarely agree on anything. The court's modern opinions are often a maze of fractured voting. Rumor has it an early justice once proposed that unanimity be required in all decisions, but they voted on it and ended up split 1-1-1-1-1-1-1-1-1. They tried to settle it with Rock, Paper,

Scissors, but one justice used real rocks and an ugly brawl broke out, after which the idea was dropped.

Perhaps it's understandable when the justices disagree about highly-charged constitutional issues like abortion or affirmative action, but they can't even agree on the most mundane matters. Consider a case like *Idaho v. Coeur d'Alene Tribe*,[39] a fight over the ownership rights to the bottom of a lake. This case was not exactly *Marbury v. Madison*, or even the lesser known *Marbury's Brother Murray v. Madison*. Yet look at the splintered voting record (this is real):

> **Kennedy, J., announced the judgment of the Court and delivered the opinion of the Court with respect to Parts I, II-A, and III, in which Rehnquist, C.J., and O'Connor, Scalia and Thomas, JJ., joined, and an opinion with respect to Parts II-B, II-C, and II-D, in which Rehnquist, C.J., joined. O'Connor, J., filed an opinion concurring in part and concurring in the judgment ....**

It goes on, but you get the idea. Way too confusing. At the end you expect to see, "See next month's opinion for answer." Readers of Supreme Court opinions need more clues to figure out these mega-part opinions, something helpful like "PLAINTIFF WINS."

Unfortunately, things are getting even worse. Check out the voting lineup in this just-decided case:

---

[39] 521 U.S. 261 (1997).

Kennedy, J., announced the judgment of the Court in which no one agreed except Mrs. Kennedy and even she wasn't too crazy about parts of it. Scalia, J., booed.

Rehnquist, C.J., dissented vigorously from Part XXXVII-A,E,I,O,UandsometimesY-*iiiiiiiii* until informed there was no such part, so he wrote his own and unleashed a vicious assault against it.

Breyer, J., concurred in Part II-A, dissented from Part II-B, was mildly amused by Part II-C, wadded up Part II-D and stuck it under his desk to keep it from rocking and used Part II-E to make paper airplanes that he and Thomas, J., shot down with rubber bands. Ginsburg, J., joined in the dissent from Part II-E so she'd have paper for her own planes.

Stevens, J., dissented, changed his mind and dissented from his dissent. On petition for reconsideration, he dissented from the dissent to his dissent, at which point he lost track of which side he wanted to win and abstained.

O'Connor, J., concurred in part in footnote six, dissenting from it not being numbered seven. Souter, J., dissented from O'Connor's partial concurrence, stating: "The issue of whether footnote six should be renumbered was not raised in the trial court and is not properly before the Court." O'Connor then filed a Supplemental Dissent canceling her RSVP to Souter's dinner party on Saturday.

4. How to Pronounce "Certiorari." Most of the cases the Supreme Court decides come to the Court via a "petition for a writ of certiorari." Law students, lawyers and probably even Supreme Court justices struggle with how to pronounce this word correctly. Since no one is really sure how to pronounce it, everyone just calls them "cert" petitions. But if you really want to stand out in a crowd, practice with this phonetic spelling: sir-sure-RARE´-ee.[40] If you REALLY want to stand out in a crowd, practice naked at a shopping mall with a microphone and a stack of Marshall® amps.

Children's Rights

Children's rights is a popular issue these days, especially among politicians. Trumpeting children's rights is an easy, economical way to make yourself appear to be a better human being than you actually are. A primary reason for the issue's popularity is that it is the only argument in America that cannot be publicly opposed. A person cannot stand up and proclaim "I oppose children's rights." Such a person would be reviled, especially by children.

Politicians have come to believe that any position can be sold to the American people as long as the word "children" is worked into it, as demonstrated by this recent argument on the House floor in favor of new subsidies for tobacco farmers:

---

[40] As with everything else in the law, there's a split of authority on the correct pronunciation, with approximately 32 percent of lawyers saying: sir-sure-ROAR´-eye.

I LOVE CHILDREN. What we need in this country is more tobacco and smoking by all age groups. AREN'T CHILDREN FANTASTIC? A vote for my bill is a vote for thousands of metric tons of additional carcinogens in the air and A VOTE FOR CHILDREN. We need to buck up and just learn to live with a lot more cancer in our society. Speaking of live, LONG LIVE THE KIDS OF AMERICA. Sure, 400,000 smoking-related deaths a year sounds like a lot. But we have a whole lot more than 400,000 PRECIOUS CHILDREN in this great nation of ours.

In this climate, children have acquired dozens of new rights. Children's rights advocates have won several recent lawsuits, including landmark decisions recognizing a fourteenth amendment substantive due process right of bodily autonomy to refuse the forced feeding of vegetables and an inalienable right to pursue happiness by jumping into mud puddles.

I'm not convinced we need to be so solicitous of children's legal rights. Having a child of my own, I'm convinced that many children are more than capable of handling their own legal problems. Children have an almost instinctive sense of the law. This most likely derives from their pervasive experience with the adversarial system, which begins at birth. By the time a child is able to walk, she has been enjoined more than 200,000 times. Every movement, every reflex, every instinctive reaction is met with injunction: "No! Don't bite. Don't touch. No! No! Don't hit. Don't pull. Spit that out. No!"

Rather than worrying about protecting children's rights, lawyers would be better off learning from the legal strategies of children.

The Case of Suzy Spikes

Consider the case of Suzy Spikes. Suzy is a precocious preadolescent girl who is close friends with my daughter, Caitlin. They play together when Suzy is not busy preparing for hearings in juvenile court. Suzy has taught Caitlin many lessons about life, most of which concern how to beat the rap.

During a recent neighborhood gathering, Suzy added a new twist to the popular childhood taunt, "Liar, liar, pants on fire." Parents listened with delight to the gleeful laughter of children ringing through the autumn air until the fire engines drowned it out.

Suzy received a speedy trial for this offense from her parents, Art and June Spikes, before whom she has successfully argued hundreds of cases. However, in this case her defense was hampered by an evidentiary ruling to "Not say even one word while I'm speaking to you, Young Lady." The sentencing phase of her proceeding provides valuable lessons for law students and lawyers:

> **An accused has the right to speak in mitigation of punishment.** Suzy asserts she's an innocent victim of the system and recounts her wounded childhood. She reminds the judges that she's always been their "precious

little puddin'" and "snuggly-wuggly-bug." She extolls the many months of patience she showed during her mother's pregnancy and asks for the same consideration. In summation, she attempts to bribe the judges. Her allocution, though impassioned, leaves the judges unmoved.

A prior record can prejudice the accused. In response, Mrs. Spikes raises Suzy's recent convictions on 23 counts of Negligent Failure to Make Bed, 47 counts of Willful Annoyance and 1,205 counts of Bad Attitude with Intent to Act Like a Teenager, a felony. At this point, a baggie falls out of Suzy's pocket and a pending charge of Unlawful Possession of Jolly Ranchers is added. Suzy objects to the introduction of this character evidence. Her objection is overruled, but she has preserved grounds for an appeal.

Never antagonize the court during sentencing. When pitiful sobbing fails to bring mercy, Suzy switches tactics to aggressive advocacy. She denounces the "corrupt judges of this kangaroo court" for their perceived inability to "never possibly know in a million years" the pressures faced by 11-year-old girls. To emphasize her point, she throws up on the carpet. This error in trial strategy results in a stiff upward adjustment under mandatory sentencing guidelines

recently adopted by the Spikes household. Suzy is currently due to be released from her room in her junior year of college.

In future editions of *The Law School Trip*, we will continue tracking this interesting case through appeal, Suzy's adolescence, first date, sixteenth birthday and hard time in the penitentiary.

Gun Control

Gun control is becoming an issue of increasing prominence in legal education. Just the other day I observed a group of students engaged in a lively debate with their Constitutional Law professor over the proper interpretation of the Second Amendment. Their arguments were quite persuasive, as was their pistol-whipping. The professor not only agreed with their position, but handed over his wallet.

The three rules of real estate are "location, location, location." The three rules of gun control debate are "statistics, statistics, statistics." To participate effectively in any discussion of gun control, you need to be able to cite statistics. They don't have to be true or accurate. To the contrary, many of the best statistics in the gun control debate aren't accurate. The key is to always one-up your opponent with a better-sounding statistic. Here's a typical gun control debate:

Gun Control Proponent: Last year in Japan, only one person was killed by a gun, while in the U.S. more than seventeen million people were killed just from getting hit in the head with ejecting shell cartridges.

Gun Control Opponent: Japan is a very regimented society. Only one Japanese citizen out of a hundred thousand gets to experience the excitement of dodging gunfire. Besides, every day in America, twenty million people use guns in self-defense and millions more use them to safeguard the country from British invasion.

Proponent: Nonsense. Studies show a gun in the home is one-hundred and forty-six million times more likely to be used to kill a snail darter than for self-defense.

Opponent: Pro-gun control statistics are one billion times stupider than anti-gun control statistics.

Proponent: If you laid all the preposterous claims of gun control opponents end to end, they would circle the universe for infinity.

Opponent: Statistically speaking, non-gun owners are six-and-a-half trillion times uglier than gun owners.

Proponent: There's a 99.99 percent chance that the rude remark I'm about to make concerning your mother will cause the veins in

your neck to explode.

Opponent: My machine gun can pump bullets into your abdomen at a gazillion-bajillion rounds per second.

Unfortunately, at this point, the quality of the debate usually begins to deteriorate.

There you have them: four hot issues you need to know to be an intelligent-sounding law student or lawyer. The more topics you can work into one conversation, the more impressive you'll sound. Just don't make the mistake of arguing that Supreme Court justices who oppose gun control should be buckled into defective Ford Pintos because your kid says so.

12

GETTING A JOB

ventually you will graduate from law school and, unless you can think of another graduate program to attend, you'll have to find a job. Fortunately, law degrees are extremely versatile. The law isn't just for lawyers anymore. Law school classrooms are jammed with people who have no intention of practicing law. Doctors, bankers, homemakers—a wide variety of people seek a Juris Doctor degree to aid them in their existing careers. Wisely so. In our complex, heavily regulated society, a law degree is becoming an increasingly vital job qualification in many fields outside the traditional practice of law. Just yesterday I came across this classified ad:

IMMEDIATE OPENINGS!
CONVENIENCE STORE CLERKS

Competitive salary and benefits. No experience necessary. Job requirements: U.S. visa, no criminal record, law degree (law review and top 10 percent only). Contact Mr. ████████

Opportunities for lawyers are usually pretty good, so you shouldn't have too much trouble finding a real legal

job. But there's bad news too. They may have forgotten to mention this to you in law school, but being a lawyer is no picnic. Forget any image you have of filthy rich lawyers lounging around on yachts sloshing down margaritas. Filthy rich lawyers work extremely hard while sloshing down margaritas.

Seriously, lawyering is a stressful job requiring long hours. In return for starting annual salaries exceeding $100,000 in major cities, associates at big law firms are expected to bill between 2,000 and 2,400 hours each year. Setting aside two weeks for vacation (don't bother), that comes out to 40 to 48 hours per week. Perhaps that doesn't sound too bad. You might be thinking, "Hmmm. That works out to eight to ten hours a day, five days a week. Not cushy, but doable. I'll spend my free nights and weekends cruising in the Porsche I buy with the money."

If you're thinking that, stop it. We're talking *billable* hours—time you're permitted to actually charge to clients. Reaching 40 to 48 billable hours a week requires a WHOLE LOT MORE real time hours. You can forget about those nights and weekends. Forget about vacations. Forget your friends, family, significant other(s), pets, hobbies, fetishes, forget everything. You're going to be too busy accounting for every moment of your existence on the dreaded DAILY TIME SHEET. As an associate at a law firm, every second of your life must be documented for billing purposes and subsequent painstaking review by workaholic partners.

Billable hours are probably the single most wretched

aspect of the practice of law. Each time you make an entry on your daily time sheet, you'll obsess simultaneously about five things: (1) whether you're getting in enough billable hours to meet the minimum annual quota; (2) how many hours the associate in the office next to you is billing; (3) whether a partner reviewing the time sheet will brand you as a drain on the firm for putting in only 10-hour days; (4) whether the common law defense of "Justification" is a viable defense to an indictment for inflating billable hours; and (5) whether you should eject yourself from the 37th-floor window.

Here's an actual daily time sheet for a new associate at a large law firm:

DAILY TIME SHEET

Time	Task	Billable Hours
7:00 am - 8:00	Attend firm meeting on strategies for boosting	
	billable hours/listen to partners' war stories.	0
8:00 - 8:01	Get coffee/chat with other associates.	0
8:02 - 8:03:	Urinate.	0
8:04 - 8:10	Sit down to work on *Billingsly* case.	.1
8:10 - 10:30	Drop everything to work on partner's speech	
	for seminar presentation in Vail.	0
10:30 - 11:00	Drive to law library to research *Billingsly* case.	0
11:00 - 11:30	Research *Billingsly* case.	.5
11:30 - 11:35	Copy research for *Billingsly* case.	.1
11:35 - 12:00	Copy machine jams/try to fix.	0

12:00 pm - 1:30	Mandatory lunch with partners/listen to war	
	stories and complaints about low billable hours.	0
1:30 - 1:33	Call spouse/get coffee/urinate.	0
1:34 - 2:00	Drive back to library.	0
2:00 - 2:30	Continue researching *Billingsly* case.	.5
2:30 - 2:35	Get "URGENT" message from partner to return	
	to firm for emergency research.	0
2:35 - 3:15	Race back to firm/ignore flashing police lights/take	
	high-speed evasive measures/flip car in near fatal	
	crash/get beaten senseless by police officers/escape	
	after wounding officer in foot with his own weapon.	0
3:15 - 3:30	Arrive back at firm bleeding from mouth with three	
	broken ribs and lacerated kidney/sprint to partner's	
	office/inquire about emergency/get assignment to	
	research legitimacy of Cayman Island tax shelter	
	partner is considering for investment.	0
3:30 - 4:30	Research real estate law in Cayman Islands	
	— curse partner.	0
4:30 - 5:00	Drive back to law library/curse partner.	0
5:00 - 5:30	Resume researching *Billingsly* case/curse partner.	.7
5:30 - 6:30	Mandatory happy hour with partners/listen to war	
	stories and complaints about low billable	
	hours/curse partners.	0
6:30 - 7:00	Drive back to law library.	0
7:00 - 7:05	Finish copying research for *Billingsly* case.	.1
7:05 - 8:15	Copy machine jams/try to fix.	0
8:15 - 8:45	Dismantle copy machine with fire ax.	0
8:45 - 9:30	Fill out time sheet.	0
	Total Billable Hours	**2.0**

If you're more interested in quality of life than big bucks, consider working for the government. Federal, state and local governments employ thousands of lawyers. Like all government employees, government lawyers have a good thing going. They get decent pay, good hours and terrific benefits. Best of all, government employees never have to worry about being fired. Job skills considered important in the private sector—things like competence, attitude and work attendance—are not requirements for many government jobs. In part, we have our great legal system to thank for this. One reason government employees seldom get fired is a fear of lawsuits.

Judged by the number of complaints filed by discharged government workers, no government employee in history has ever been fired for a legitimate reason. Every pink-slipped bureaucrat since the Jefferson administration apparently has been the victim of a scientifically aberrant cluster of malevolent persons holding supervisory positions in government agencies.

You might as well send out an invitation to a lawsuit when firing a government worker in today's litigious society. Indeed, to increase efficiency, the federal government has begun doing just that. The Code of Federal Regulations was recently amended to include **Form 458793480-2984-895, Invitation to Lawsuit for Discharged Federal Employees**:

You're Invited!!!

<u>To What</u>: *A lawsuit claiming we discriminated against you based on your gender, age, ethnicity, disability, religion, inability to function as a competent human being, alcohol addiction, absenteeism, workplace brawling, weapon brandishing or (other)_____.*

<u>Why</u>: *You've been reassigned from your position as (fill in)* <u>U.S. POSTAL WORKER</u> *to unemployment.*

<u>Where</u>: *We'll meet for a short reception at the Equal Employment Opportunity Commission before carpooling to federal court.*

<u>Who's Invited</u>: *All your former supervisors and colleagues.*

<u>What to bring</u>: *Allegations, subpoenas, expert witnesses, credibility. (Do not bring assault weapon unless you checked box for Alternative Dispute Resolution Option B.)*

<u>Dress</u>: *Suitable business attire.*

The Résumé

Whether you decide on the public or private sector, you need to pay attention to marketing yourself properly. Image is everything in America. In the legal field, successful marketing requires a good résumé. Follow the suggestions below and you have my personal Lifetime Guarantee[41] that you will find a job.

Never be modest when compiling a resume. Believe in yourself. Put your best foot forward. Compose a résumé that shouts "HIRE ME!" (Let the resume do the talking. Don't you shout "HIRE ME!" Shouting is considered a bad interviewing technique.) I know what some of you are thinking: "My credentials are terrible. There's no way to make them shout anything other than, 'I'M DOOMED!'" Relax. There are two proven strategies for handling less-than-stellar résumé credentials.

Tweaking Approach. The first is tweaking. A little creative embellishment can do wonders for anyone's credentials. Tweaking is not the same as lying, which is forbidden. Tweaked credentials must bear at least a tenuous connection to reality. To better grasp this technique, compare some weak credentials with some tweaked credentials:

---

[41] LIMITED LIFETIME GUARANTEE. AUTHOR GUARANTEES READER WILL FIND SOME KIND OF JOB AT SOME POINT IN HIS OR HER LIMITED LIFETIME OR WILL RETURN PURCHASE MONEY MINUS AMOUNT ALREADY SPENT TO READER'S ESTATE UPON PRESENTATION OF CERTIFIED DEATH CERTIFICATE BY READER.

Grade Point Average

Weak Credential: GPA: 2.09

Tweaked Credential: My grades were way above the norm. (If challenged on this later, say you meant way above "Norm," the guy who sat next to you in Commercial Paper.)

Law Review Status

Weak Credential: None.

Tweaked Credential: I came very close to making the editor-in-chief. (To establish a foundation for this statement, ask the editor-in-chief out on a date and pray s/he finds you attractive.)

Legal Experience

Weak Credential: Got sued by Blockbuster® for not returning rented videos.

Tweaked Credential: Set precedent in blockbuster intellectual property case.

Hobbies and Interests

Weak Credential: Sleeping, drinking beer and watching *Seinfeld* reruns.

Tweaked Credential: Energy conservation, doing grassroots work to support America's grain farmers and studying urban social interaction.

Brutal Honesty Approach. At the opposite end of the continuum from tweaking is complete honesty. Some hiring partners, usually those in therapy, find soul-baring to be endearing. Here's a model to work with:

RÉSUMÉ OF DARREN "DROOPY" DRIPP

OBJECTIVE:

Finding a place to work where everyone doesn't hate me and no one reminds me of my mother. I'm seeking a friendly work environment where social interaction among employees, especially sexual intercourse, is encouraged. The hours must be flexible to give me time to work on my novel. As far as location, proximity to a liquor store is a consideration.

LEGAL EDUCATION:

Brickyard School of Law (Anticipated Graduation Date: ???) — My graduation is currently in question due to my inability to perform well on law school exams. I've pondered the reasons for this for three years and have decided the most plausible explanation is my low IQ. However, my therapist says the fact that several of my professors remind me of my mother is also a hindrance.

EMPLOYMENT EXPERIENCE:

Mega-Food Supermarket — Job responsibilities: took cans out of boxes and put them on shelves; swept floor; cleaned up broken condiment bottles. Reason for leaving: Medical emergency when 20 pounds of Alaskan King Crab legs I was shoplifting punctured my testicular sac.

Green Thumb Nursery — Job responsibilities: applied water to plants. Supervisor said I showed "excellent initiative." Reason for leaving: Nursery filed for bankruptcy after plants died from overwatering.

Stop 'N Pop Convenience Store — Job responsibilities: sold beer and cigarettes, mostly to minors. Reason for leaving: same as above.

Whatever strategy you select, always have your résumé printed on really thick beige stationary. The weaker your credentials, the thicker the paper should be.

The Recommendation Letter

Never are a law professor's words more highly valued than when students come seeking letters of recommendations. These letters can help a lot in the job search process, so don't be shy about asking for one. Most professors are happy to help further the careers of their students.

Students at the top of the class have no problem getting glowing recommendation letters. Neither do middle-of-the-packers who are perceived by their professors as competent, hard workers. However, there are always those problem cases, students for whom writing a good letter of recommendation can be a daunting, even painful, challenge. Maybe you're one of these students. But don't worry. Look what a law professor was able to do for Harold Weenicker:

BRICKYARD SCHOOL OF LAW
Laying Legal Foundations for More Than A Century

June 30, 2001

Ms. Laura Keenbeam, Managing Partner
Keenbeam, Broadbaum & Finch, P.A.
600 Capital Suite Plaza
Chicago, Illinois 60611

Re: Job Application of Harold Weenicker

Dear Ms. Keenbeam:

Harold Weenicker, a former student of mine, is applying for an associate position with your firm and asked me to write a letter of recommendation on his behalf.

During his law school career, Mr. Weenicker was enrolled in several of my courses, most of which he completed. In those he did, he always showed up for the final exam, occasionally on time. While his grades were somewhat below average, his essay answers were always very creative. In fact, Harold informs me his Torts exam is due to be published in a Gothic short story anthology.

Mr. Weenicker truly distinguished himself in Constitutional Law. In a class of more than 100 students, he talked the most.

Mr. Weenicker is assertive and capable of strongly defending his positions, as he demonstrated during a spirited discussion of *Martin v. Hunter's Lessee*. I was particularly impressed by his ability to jab and circle to his left. However, Harold can also be a pleasure to be around, particularly when he is taking his medication.

It is my understanding that a major portion of your firm's practice is in the area of criminal defense. Thus, Mr. Weenicker's two felony convictions may actually prove to be

an asset, given his "real world" experience with the rules of criminal procedure. The same goes for your domestic relations practice. Harold's recent divorce, which you may have read about in the papers, would seem to make him a natural fit.

Reviewing Mr. Weenicker's résumé, one cannot help but be impressed by the variety of extracurricular activities he participated in while in law school. Truthfully, I did not know our law school had a chapter of Students for a Law-Free Society until Mr. Weenicker successfully campaigned for the presidency.

His strong commitment to social justice is reflected in his reliable participation in our Habitat for Humanity projects, where he never failed to bring the beer. And certainly, his recognition in Who's Who Among College Students from Natchez, Mississippi and listing in the American Directory of Genitalia-Piercers warrant praise.

In short, I can state with confidence that a decision to hire Mr. Weenicker could possibly turn out not badly.

I would be happy to provide additional information regarding Harold Weenicker, but will be tied up for the next six years, so you may wish to contact someone else. I understand his supervisor in the Witness Protection Program speaks highly of him.

Sincerely,

Joseph P. Bugler

Joseph P. Bugler
Professor of Law

P.S. Frankly, I believe Mr. Weenicker's role in the recent incident leading to the Dean's early retirement and closing of the law school for two months has been exaggerated.

The Interview

Once you've put together an appealing résumé and extracted a letter of recommendation from one of your professors, the next step is the interview. Be prepared for the worst when you go into a legal job interview. Legal employers are notorious for asking impossible questions that have no good answers. According to Kimm Alayne Walton's excellent book, *Guerrilla Tactics For Getting the Legal Job of Your Dreams*, they do this not so much because they want to know the answer as to test your ability to handle pressure. So when an interviewer asks "What's your greatest weakness?," avoid honest answers like "Life terrifies me" or "I hate the law."

Walton wisely advises job applicants to prepare answers to tough questions in advance, but if she's right about employers intentionally putting us on the spot, a more aggressive response may be called for. People are stressed out enough at job interviews. We don't need interviewers trying to make us look bad. As Americans, we enjoy the basic, inalienable right to do that for ourselves.

Fight back with the new interviewing strategy especially designed with today's pugnacious young lawyer in mind: INTIMIDATION. Answer all tough questions with the goal of making the employer afraid NOT to hire you. For example, if an interviewer asks, "Do you have what it takes to bring business into the firm?," respond, "Of course. It's in the trunk of my car. Just tell me whose business you want."

Here are some of the toughest legal job interview questions and some intimidating *Gorilla* Tactics for answering them:

Q. Tell us about yourself.

A. *Which one? Fred's been bad. He can't come out today.*

Q. Did you get into any other law schools?

A. *Plenty. In fact, I got into every Ivy League school except Columbia. Now there's a school that deserves its top ranking. It has the finest alarm system in the nation.*

Q. What's your greatest weakness?

A. *Thirst for vengeance. I've spent years in therapy battling it, but I always end up trying to get even with my inner child.*

Q. Where do you see yourself five years from now?

A. *As a highly-paid member of your firm or possibly at the Super-Max Federal Correctional Facility.*

Q. Why didn't you get an offer from your last employer?

A. *I might have. It was hard to understand what he was yelling from behind the locked door.*

Q. Why aren't your grades better?

A. *Because my professors, like most people around me, possibly including you, are engaged in a conspiracy to persecute me unjustly.*

Q. What's your greatest strength?

A. *I can carry a rocket-propelled grenade launcher in one hand.*

Q. Who else are you interviewing with?

A. *I've received several offers, but they're not legal positions, at least not in this country.*

Q. Why should we hire you?

A. *Ha, ha, ha, ha, ha, ha, ha, ha, ha, ha, ha, ha ...*

Obviously, this strategy is not for everyone. It's only for the criminally insane. For everyone else, I suggest sticking with the advice in *Guerrilla Tactics*.

13

POST

MORTEM

THE BAR EXAM
& OTHER THINGS
TO WORRY ABOUT

raduation day! A time of jubilation, liberation, celebration—for 15 minutes, after which you have to hunker down and start studying for the bar exam. Perhaps the most heartbreaking aspect of law school is that the only thing more stressful than attending is actually graduating.[42]

The bar exam is two days of hell that will make an ordinary law school exam seem like a first-grade quiz on words that rhyme with "hat." It's a grueling affair covering almost every subject you had in law school and some you didn't. It includes loads of essay questions, plus the Multistate Bar Examination®, also known as The 200 Worst Multiple Choice Questions Ever Written®. Adding insult and financial hardship to misery, to have any hope of passing you'll have to pay a thousand dollars for a commercial "bar review course" during which you will learn much of the law for the first time.

Reader: What's he talking about, "learn the law for the first time"? What about the three years I spent in law school? My eyes must be getting tired. I'll have to re-read that last sentence. Probably a typo.

Sorry. You read it right. Some schools do not teach students what they need to know to pass the bar exam.

---

[42] This is only a test to see if you're still reading your footnotes. Had this been a real footnote, you would have been instructed to turn to your *Bluebook* for further obfuscation. I repeat, this is only a test.

Remember, the best schools teach you to *think about* the law. Schools that are seen as teaching students to pass the bar exam are looked down on in legal education. But even at schools that actually teach the law, students can't possibly learn every subject tested on modern bar exams because the BAR EXAMINERS HAVE GONE CRAZY in testing applicants on dozens of subject areas most students will never encounter in real life and that the bar examiners themselves know zilch about. I firmly believe that an afterlife exists in which law students who lead good and decent lives will get to pass time watching conference halls full of bar examiners sweat, squirm and pee in their pants while trying to write passing answers to essay questions about Commercial Paper and Secured Transactions.

The good news is that commercial bar review courses, though expensive, can teach you the entire universe of law in only six weeks. Bar review books are worth their weight in gold. These are the true genius treatises in all of law. However, even with a review course, the bar exam is a terrible, terrible thing. I'd be lying if I said otherwise. Lucky for you, I remember the pep talk one of my professors shared with me back when I was studying for the bar exam:

> Relax. It's just another test. Keep it in perspective. Don't let the fact that YOUR ENTIRE LIFE depends on passing make you nervous. So what if you FAIL? Feelings of FAILURE AND WORTHLESSNESS can be dealt with by qualified MENTAL HEALTH PROFESSIONALS. They have excellent MEDICATION these days for DEPRES-SION. Don't worry about how you're going to

PAY BACK YOUR STUDENT LOANS if you FAIL. The government is unlikely to SUE YOU if your law firm FIRES YOU because you FAILED the bar exam. As for supporting yourself, there are plenty of JOBS IN THE FOOD SERVICE SECTOR. And remember, you can always TAKE THE BAR EXAM AGAIN. So just relax.

Feel better? Good.

It probably seems impossible, but it's *after* you pass the bar exam that the real worries start because now you have to actually practice law. There's a good reason it's called "practicing law." Like most things in life, the law takes practice. But in law school, you only get to *think about* practicing law, unless you enroll in what is known as a "live client clinic" where you get to represent real people.[43] Fortunately, practice makes perfect. After about 5,000 near misses and a few direct hits with malpractice, you'll be fine.

In addition to the fear of getting sued for malpractice, you'll find lots of other new stresses such as keeping track of billable hours, giving up your weekends, finding clients (and watching the partners take credit for it), reporting to clients, holding clients' hands, kissing the lower rear portion of clients' anatomy, losing clients (and watching the partners blame you for it), planning a vacation for a year and having to cancel it because your adversary scheduled a deposition for the exact moment you were scheduled to be applying suntan lotion in Bermuda, filling out labyrinthine expense reports, feeling inadequate

---

[43] If you're interested in wills and trusts, consider petitioning the dean to start a "dead client clinic."

because your secretary knows 1,000 times (very conservative estimate) as much about the practice of law as you do, keeping up with law firm personnel turnover and who actually does what at any given hour of the day, keeping track of who hates whom in the firm, being instructed by partners to go find good law supporting your client's position when it doesn't exist and then suffering their tirades because you lack the magical ability to alter the common law, living at the mercy of the photocopy machine repair person, witnessing the crash of your firm's computer network a half hour before the filing deadline for a 50-page brief, enduring the tyranny of entrenched lifers, trying to explain to a client who has been paying you $150 per hour why you lost his case, wasting precious billable hours serving on firm committees, writing speeches and articles for partners who take all the credit, battling pro se litigants who learned the law from Judge Judy, and much, much more. But this is all the subject of another book, if I'm lucky.

Speaking of books, I hope you found this one enlightening. I also hope you found it entertaining. Mostly, I'm just glad you found it.

My final words may surprise you. Contrary to the impression that may have been created in these pages, all the stress and insanity of law school are well worth it. Why? Because being a lawyer can be a very rewarding profession. For one thing, the law is interesting, which is a whole lot more than can be said about most professions. Sure, doctors make a lot more money, but, let's face it, a spleen is a spleen. If you've seen one, you've seen them all, and according to the Medicaid

records of a few doctors, removed them all.

But the law is always fresh and interesting. Why? Because its horizons are limited only by the ability of human beings to behave properly, rationally and legally. In other words, there are no limits at all. As a result, the law pervades every aspect of human existence. To quote a great song by the Police, "Every slip we make, every fall we take, every bone we break"—they all have legal implications. No human act is too trivial to be eliminated as a potential basis for invoking the American legal system. You're probably saying, "You're wrong, McClurg. I can think of lots of trivial human acts that can be eliminated as a potential basis for invoking the American legal system."

I thought you'd say that, so I've included some examples to prove my point. Look at the potential legal implications of these mundane daily acts:

Mundane Act: Blinking.
Legal implications: "Visual abuse" sexual harassment claim.
Mundane Act: Breathing.
Legal Implications: Violate EPA air quality standards.
Mundane Act: Thinking.
Legal Implications: Ground for employment termination if government worker.
Mundane Act: Doodling.
Legal Implications: Tattoo parlor shut down by cease and desist order.

Mundane Act:	Inserting videotape.
Legal Implications:	Sodomy charges.

All joking aside, lawyering remains one of the noblest of all professions. Lawyers are the true champions of our freedom. Lawyers wrote the Constitution and have defended it for more than 200 years. History has shown time and again that lawyers are among the only ones who can be counted on to fight for liberty when it's unpopular to do so. We aren't perfect, but as a fellow named Harrison Tweed once said: "With all their faults, [lawyers] stack up well against those in every other occupation or profession. They are better to work with or play with or fight with or drink with than most other varieties of mankind." Be proud to be a law student and a lawyer. Don't let the jibes get to you. The same people telling lawyer jokes will be the first to call you when they get in trouble.

Phew. Being serious for an entire paragraph is exhausting, so enough of that. There are at least 10 other great reasons to be a lawyer:

TEN GREAT REASONS TO BE A LAWYER

10. You can get more than 2,000 credit cards.

9. You have a legitimate reason to put your picture above restroom urinals.

8. You won't have to pay expensive attorney's fees in the event of an ugly divorce.

7. You don't have to worry about not having anything to do on weekends.

6. You can come home from a long, exhausting day practicing law, flip on the TV, kick back and watch 10 shows about practicing law.

5. You can scare the hell out of your doctor just by filling in "Occupation" on your patient form.

4. You get to put the letters "J.D." after your name, which if you slip in an "e" and an "i" makes you a JeDi.

3. You have an excuse for why people don't like you that has nothing to do with your sorry personality or revolting personal habits.

2. You get to say "I'm a lawyer" when you meet someone in a bar.

1. You get to sue people.

So that's the complete law school trip, and then some. Now that you've read the whole story, you can see why this book is indispensable. KEEP IT IN YOUR BACK POCKET AT ALL TIMES. It will provide insight in the darkness of confusion, bolster your will to fight the forces that would thwart you and can stop a .25 caliber bullet if you get shot in the buttocks during a drive-by.

PRODUCT WARNING: FOR JOKING PURPOSES ONLY. DO NOT LET YOURSELF GET SHOT IN THE BUTTOCKS. IT WILL RUIN THE BOOK, AS WELL AS YOUR BUTTOCKS, WHICH PROBABLY DON'T LOOK THAT GREAT TO BEGIN WITH.

Good luck![44]

---

[44] Ha. Thought I was done, didn't you? As I said way back on the first page in footnote 1, the whole purpose of legal footnotes is to allow a thought to continue indefinitely. I'm just getting my second wind. Now I'm finally going to reveal to you the single most important secret of law school. Ready? Here it is. The most important secret of law school is—ack—what's this in the mail? A cease and desist letter from an intellectual property law firm!!! You're not going to believe this. It turns out The Most Important Secret of Law School® is a Registered Trade Secret®.

So sorry.

About the Author

Photo: Dixie Knight

Andrew J. McClurg is a professor at Florida International University College of Law, and has previously taught law at the University of Arkansas at Little Rock, the University of Colorado, Golden Gate University, and Wake Forest University. A well-known "serious" scholar in the areas of tort law and firearms policy, McClurg has won several awards both for his teaching and publications. His academic articles have been cited by numerous state and federal courts and in more than 100 different law reviews. His co-edited book, *Gun Control and Gun Rights*, was recently published by the New York University Press.

McClurg grew up in Hollywood, Florida, where he misspent his youth playing pinball at the beach and cruising around listening to eight-track tapes at high volume. He graduated from the University of Florida with degrees in journalism and law and an unhealthy obsession with the Florida Gator football team. After law school, he worked as a judicial law clerk for a federal judge and four years as a trial lawyer before entering academia.

Although he's been trying to get laughs since he was *in utero*, McClurg's professional career as a humorist began on a steamy summer afternoon in 1995 when, frustrated by the strictures of academic writing, he exited a footnote and dashed off *The World's Greatest Law Review Article*, a heavily-footnoted parody of real law review articles. The parody struck a chord with readers and led to *Harmless Error: A Truly Minority View on the Law*, his off-beat humor column for lawyers and law students that appeared monthly in the *American Bar Association Journal* from 1997-2001. In 2001, McClurg started *lawhaha.com*, an award-winning legal humor Web site. He also performs stand-up legal humor for bar conventions and other lawyer gatherings and is co-editor of a forthcoming anthology of legal humor.

McClurg has been quoted as a humorist by sources such as the Associated Press and CNN.com, and as a legal expert by National Public Radio, *Time*, *U.S. News & World Report*, the *New York Times*, *Washington Post*, *National Law Journal*, *Miami Herald*, *Los Angeles Times*, *Chicago Tribune*, *San Francisco Chronicle*, *Newsday*, and many other sources.

E-mail McClurg at mcclurga@fiu.edu.

ISBN 1552126463

9 781552 126462